EX LIBRIS

A SUSSEX GUIDE

SUSSEX MUSIC

MARCUS WEEKS

INTRODUCED BY
GAVIN HENDERSON

Illustrated by
MADDY McCLELLAN

SNAKE RIVER PRESS

SNAKE RIVER PRESS

Book No 11
Books about Sussex for the enthusiast

Published in 2008 by
SNAKE RIVER PRESS
South Downs Way, Alfriston, Sussex BN26 5XW
www.snakeriverpress.co.uk

ISBN 978-1-906022-10-5

This book was conceived, designed and produced by
SNAKE RIVER PRESS

Copyright © Snake River Press Limited 2008
Text © Marcus Weeks
Illustration © Maddy McClellan

All rights reserved. No part of this book may be reproduced
in any form without written permission from the publisher.

The publishers and authors have done their best to ensure
the accuracy and currency of all information at the date of preparation.
Readers who intend to rely on the information to undertake any activity
should check the current accuracy. The publishers and authors accept
no responsibility for any loss, injury or inconvenience sustained by the
reader as a result of information or advice contained in this book.

ART DIRECTOR & PUBLISHER *Peter Bridgewater*
EDITORIAL DIRECTOR *Viv Croot*
EDITOR *Rob Yarham*
PAGE MAKEUP *Richard Constable & Chris Morris*
ILLUSTRATOR *Maddy McClellan*
CONSULTANT *Lorraine Harrison*

This book is typeset in Perpetua & Gill Sans,
two fonts designed by Eric Gill

Printed and bound in China

DEDICATION

To Dad, who loved Sussex and music

CONTENTS

FOREWORD 6

INTRODUCTION 8

SUSSEX BY THE SEA 10

SUSSEX FOLK MUSIC 12

THE BROADWOOD
    COLLECTION 14

HORSHAM FOLK 16

MEET THE COPPERS 18

SUSSEX SONGSHEET 22

THE SUSSEX REVIVAL 24

MEET THE FOLK 26

CLASSICAL SUSSEX 28

THOMAS WEELKES 30

VAUGHAN WILLIAMS & BAX . .34

JOHN IRELAND 36

LAST NIGHT OF THE PROMS . .38

PERCY GRAINGER 40

FRANK BRIDGE 42

MUSICAL OPINION 44

MICHAEL TIPPETT 46

HAVERGAL BRIAN 48

PROGRESSIVE
    v CONSERVATIVE 50

SUSSEX ACADEME 54

MICHAEL FINNISSY 56

SUSSEX VIRTUOSI 58

CLASSICAL BEAUTIES 60

WINIFRED WAGNER 62

SUSSEX ENSEMBLES 64

SUSSEX POP 66

VARIETY PERFORMERS 68

JAZZ 70

LIGHTS, CAMERA, ACTION . . .72

ROCK & POP 74

BRIAN JONES 76

A GOOD NIGHT OUT 78

PERFORMING HERITAGE . .80

GLYNDEBOURNE 82

DE LA WARR PAVILION 86

BRIGHTON DOME 88

ST MARY-IN-THE-CASTLE 90

END-OF-THE-PIER SHOW 92

FESTIVALS, FURTHER
    READING & WEBSITES 94

INDEX 95

FOREWORD

Marcus Weeks' study of music in Sussex admirably reflects the rich mix of cultures that has been woven over the centuries to form this colourful county – or, some might bureaucratically, say two counties, for East and West Sussex have very distinctive characteristics, and indeed Councils. As a coastal stretch, it has always been 'at the edge' – a busy thoroughfare, through which so many travel to and from 'abroad'; it is also an escape from the metropolis, not least as a holiday destination, and more recently as a commuter belt. But transient as much of its population may be, its Downland and Wealden landscape has sustained a truly indigenous populace, with deepseated folk traditions – particularly in music.

What follows is a tapestry of soundscape, from the ballads, songs and shanties of a Sussex that faced the frontline of the Norman Conquests, saved our monarchy in effecting the escape of Charles II, and fostered the very musical Regency of George IV, in a Brighton that welcomed visits from such luminaries as Rossini and Paganini. Its own anthem *Sussex by the Sea* resounded through the Edwardian establishment of musical entertainment at the fashionable resorts. For more than 70 years it has boasted the very pinnacle of high society in the unique pleasures of Glyndebourne Opera. Cathedral and church music abound, and where many may think that Elgar's Cello Concerto, and his three great chamber works, are steeped in the Malvern Hills – they aren't; they grew from out of the shadows of the Downs in war-torn Sussex. Other formidable composers also put down their roots here – Parry, Bridge, Bax, Ireland, Brian and Ketelbey, and more recently Tavener, Harvey, Finnissy and Blake.

Popular entertainment has flourished through 'end of the Pier' concert parties and summer shows, on the glorious sheltered bandstands (so beautifully maintained at Eastbourne and Worthing), and in the chandeliered ballrooms of innumerable fine hotels. Indeed, the original Palm Court Trio of the BBC's Grand Hotel came from the eponymous hotel in Eastbourne, which also formed the extraordinary backdrop to Debussy's La Mer. The throb of the Sixties provoked invasions of teenage mods and rockers – frenzied in their thrall to bands such as The Who – while the Beatles and the Rolling Stones made iconic appearances at Brighton's Hippodrome.

Festivals great and small now flourish in Sussex – from Brighton to Petworth. Arts centres have been established and revitalised, giving the new town of Crawley its handsome Hawth, and Bexhill its gloriously restored De La Warr Pavilion, not to mention Brighton's Dome, Corn Exchange and Old Market. Jazz and folk clubs are also thriving, and a vibrant club culture that represents the inventive pulse of a very youthful aspect sits beside the tenacious wellbeing of old established orchestral societies and music clubs. Sussex is truly a cosmopolitan and catholic musical society, so very well captured in this book.

GAVIN HENDERSON
Sussex born and bred – and Director of the Brighton Festival, 1984-1994.

INTRODUCTION

' ... a lovely place to cultivate one's egotism ... I shall have to leave,
because there are too many draughts and too much music.'

CLAUDE DEBUSSY, *LETTER FROM EASTBOURNE*

It's probably not the first county to spring to mind when thinking about
music, but as Flora Poste, heroine of Stella Gibbons's *Cold Comfort Farm*,
pointed out, 'Sussex, when all was said and done, was not quite like
other counties'. Sussex people are reputedly obstinate and not easily
impressed, but they can also be disarmingly modest – Sussex musicians
are not ones to blow their own trumpet, and can give a false im-
pression of the wealth of music in our county (yes, our county – I am one
of those Sussex musicians).

This book is an attempt to redress the balance, for once proudly
proclaiming our musical heritage and pointing out the often surprising
contribution Sussex has made to music in Britain and indeed worldwide.
Not only home-grown talent, but also as a place that has attracted
musicians from elsewhere with its inspiring landscape and straight-
forward but easy-going people.

While making no claims to be a comprehensive survey (and certainly
not a directory of venues and musicians or a guide to what's on), I hope
it gives an adequate flavour of the richness of musical life in Sussex past
and present. The book is divided into sections covering folk music, classical music, the mixed bag of popular music from music hall to rock, and
places of particular importance or interest in our musical history, such
as Glyndebourne; something for all tastes then, even allowing for changes
in fashion, and an unavoidably subjective emphasis in certain areas.

The first criterion for including people here is that they should have
been born, or have spent some significant time, in Sussex, and contributed in some way to the music of the county. The amount of space
devoted to each one, however, is not solely dictated by their musical
merit, but often simply because there's an interesting story to tell,
especially if this is characteristically Sussex; that is, endearingly

eccentric, self-effacing, or downright bloody-minded. The places, similarly, have been chosen for their interest or historical significance rather than because they are major centres of musical activity, which come and go with changes in musical taste. There is (and, it appears, always has been) a lot of music in Sussex, and what appears in the limelight often hides what's going on backstage; inevitably, some names and places will have been missed – so my apologies to anyone disappointed or slighted by any omissions, which are, I hope, due to ignorance rather than prejudice.

In the research for this book, I often tumbled on something by sheer chance. For example, a jazz-playing colleague of mine mentioned in passing that the composer and writer Cyril Scott had been a neighbour of his in Eastbourne, affectionately known as 'Uncle Cyril' and locally famous for his lime-green piano; when I expressed some surprise, he replied, 'I thought everybody knew that'. This is a typically Sussex matter-of-fact attitude to celebrity, which is possibly why musicians like it here – but frustrating for those who aren't in the know. So, sadly, a lot of local 'common knowledge' actually remains a well-kept secret, and although I may have uncovered some of the lesser known stories of music in Sussex, there are probably still more lurking in corners around the county. I'd be genuinely delighted to hear from any readers.

SUSSEX BY THE SEA

BRITAIN'S ONLY COUNTY ANTHEM

S ussex has not only inspired a great deal of music, but is also arguably unique in having its own county anthem, *Sussex by the Sea*. This stirring march song is proudly performed by 'the men from Sussex' at any opportunity – it has been adopted by the county regiment as their regimental march, and as the school march of Christ's Hospital, it is the battle cry of Brighton & Hove Albion football club and Sussex cricket team, and it is sung at many of the Sussex bonfire celebrations.

Its enduring popularity both within and beyond the bounds of the county is no doubt due to its rousing opening fanfare and tuneful chorus as much as its (admittedly rather dated) patriotic lyrics, all of which were written by William Ward-Higgs – who was, however, not actually a Sussex man. He was born in Birkenhead in 1866, and spent much of his life in London working as a solicitor, living at Hollywood House in Bersted, Bognor Regis, for only five or six years. When his favourite sister-in-law became engaged to Captain Waithman of the 2nd Battalion, Royal Sussex Regiment, Ward-Higgs decided to compose a song for the couple. He had previously set to music several of the *Barrack-Room Ballads* by Rudyard Kipling, and was probably inspired by Kipling's poem 'Sussex', which concludes with the line, 'Yea, Sussex by the sea!' The resulting paean to the county was published in 1907, and Waithman performed it in concerts at Ballykinlar Camp in Ireland where the battalion was then stationed. The men loved it, and it had become their regimental march by the time they were called upon to 'stand or fall' in World War I.

By this time, Ward-Higgs had moved to London. Suffering from epilepsy in later life, he was driven to take his own life in Roehampton in 1936, but his remains are buried, as befits the composer of the definitive Sussex anthem, in Bersted churchyard.

LYRICS TO SUSSEX BY THE SEA

VERSE 1

Now is the time for marching, now let
 your hearts be gay,
Hark to the merry bugles sounding
 along our way.
So let your voices ring my boys, and
 take the time from me,
And I'll sing you a song as we march
 along
Of Sussex by the sea!

CHORUS

Sussex, Sussex by the sea!
Good old Sussex by the sea!
You may tell them all we stand or fall
For Sussex by the sea.

VERSE 2

For we're the men from Sussex, Sussex
 by the sea.
We plough and sow and reap and mow
And useful men are we
So when you go to Sussex, whoever you
 may be,
You can tell them all that we stand
 or fall
For Sussex by the sea!

VERSE 3

Up in the morning early, start at the
 break of day,
March till the evening shadows, tell us
 it's time to stay.
We're always moving on me boys, so
 take your time from me,
And sing this song as we march along,
Of Sussex by the sea!

VERSE 4

Light is the love of a soldier; that's
 what the ladies say
Lightly he goes a wooing, lightly he
 rides away,
In love and war, we always are as fair
 as fair can be
And a soldier boy is a lady's joy
In Sussex by the sea!

VERSE 5

Far o'er the seas we soldier, wide
 through the world we roam;
Far from the kind hearts yonder, far
 from our dear old homes;
But ne'er shall we forget, my boys, and
 true we'll ever be.
To the girls so kind that we left behind
In Sussex by the sea!

VERSE 6

Sometimes your feet are weary,
 sometimes the way is long,
Sometimes the day is dreary, sometimes
 the world goes wrong.
But if you let your voices ring, your
 cares will fly away,
So we'll sing you a song as we march
 along
Of Sussex by the sea!

Sussex by the Sea

To hear the Anthem go to: www.royalsussex.org.uk/RSLHG_Music/Sussex by the Sea.mp3

PART ONE

SUSSEX FOLK MUSIC

For those who don't know the county, Sussex is often thought of as a sort of rural adjunct to London with few distinguishing features. Outsiders, or 'furriners' as they're known down here, seldom recognise that Sussex has a cultural identity as unique as any other county, with regional dialects just as impenetrable to the non-native and a wealth of traditional song. Ignorance of Sussex's heritage is probably what prompted Cecil Sharp, founder of the English Folk Dance and Song Society, to pronounce dismissively, 'Sussex is not a distinguished singing county'. Either that, or he had some prejudice against the county – because it's well short of the truth.

The old songs have been passed down by Sussex people themselves, and there's a thriving folk scene in many parts of the county. Local characters have achieved heroic status, and distinguished folk musicians have carried the torch.

Sussex is a rural county and its long coastline is peopled by fishermen as well as ice cream salesmen and hoteliers. And it's the ordinary people who create the folk tradition, so we have a large body of rustic songs and dances, and a good smattering of songs about the sea too.

But folk music in Sussex has remained a living tradition, not just a preservation of the past. The 1960s saw yet another folk song revival, in Sussex perhaps more than elsewhere, with a plethora of folk clubs and pubs rediscovering the folk heritage of the county and updating it for the pop era. Several Sussex folkies achieved almost rock-star status, and many of the trailblazers of the subsequent 'folk-rock' movement had Sussex connections. Interest has continued into the 21st century, and there's no sign of it abating.

Not a 'distinguished singing county'?

THE BROADWOOD COLLECTION

OLD ENGLISH SONGS

One of the by-products of the Romantic movement of the 19th century was a middle-class fascination with folklore, which in turn prompted the so-called 'folk revival' in Victorian Britain. The truth is that folk didn't need any revival – it was alive and kicking, as it had been for centuries – but was only just being discovered and appreciated by the educated classes.

Fearful that rural traditions and music would be lost in the accelerating industrialisation and urbanisation, a new breed of enthusiasts set out, like butterfly collectors, to track down and capture the old ways and tunes for posterity. In the vanguard of this bid to preserve our folklore were a number of clergymen who had been posted to rural parishes. In Sussex, two country parsons stand out for their efforts in this endeavour: the Reverend W. D. Parish, who was curate at Firle, and later vicar of Selmeston and Alciston, whose *Dictionary of the Sussex Dialect* was published in 1875; and the Reverend John Broadwood of Lyne House (between Rusper and Capel on the Sussex-Surrey border north of Horsham), who published his collection of *Old English Songs* in 1843 – perhaps the first such collection of traditional music.

Broadwood was the grandson of the founding father of the Broadwood piano-making business in London, and his family moved to Sussex when he was a child. Growing up in Sussex, he got to know the local songs, as he recollects in the subtitle he gave his anthology:

> as now Sung by the Peasantry of the Weald of Surrey and Sussex, and collected
> by one who has learnt them by hearing them Sung every Christmas from
> early Childhood, by The Country People, who go about to the Neighbouring
> Houses, Singing, 'Waissailing' as it is called, at that Season. The Airs are set
> to Music, exactly as they are now Sung, to rescue them from oblivion, and to

afford a specimen of genuine Old English Melody: and the words are given
in their original rough state, with an occasional slight alteration to render
the sense intelligible.

His niece, Lucy Etheldred Broadwood (*1858-1929*), followed in his footsteps, collecting songs herself from the late 1890s, and lived for a time in the Broadwood family home, Lyne House. She was a contemporary of Cecil Sharp, and shared with him a passion for folk song and a scholarly approach to the subject (she was one of the first to use the phonograph to record her findings), and the results of her research were published in the anthologies *Sussex Songs*, *English County Songs* and *English Traditional Songs & Carols*. She also helped to form the Folk Song Society in 1898 and served as its secretary and later editor of its Journal. She was honoured for her work by being elected President of the Society in 1928, just a year before her death.

Classical collectors

The Broadwoods started the ball rolling, encouraging folk-song enthusiasts such as W. Percy Merrick, George Butterworth and Francis Jekyll to explore the Sussex repertoire. Also swept along in the wave of collectors were a few 'classical' musicians, among them Percy Grainger and Ralph Vaughan Williams – who both had Sussex connections (more about them in Part Two, *see pages 40 and 34*). Grainger was rather cavalier in his appropriation of the folk melodies he had recorded from all over the world, including arrangements of old Sussex tunes such as *The Merry King* and the *Sussex Mummers' Christmas Carol*. Vaughan Williams, however, took the whole business more seriously: he knew the Broadwood collection well – he even had Lucy Broadwood sing examples at lectures he gave on English folk tunes – and was so respected as a serious and meticulous collector that the library at Cecil Sharp House is now known as the Vaughan Williams Memorial Library.

Top Places
- *Rusper churchyard, burial place of the Broadwood family*
- *Rusper church, which has a plaque dedicated to Lucy's memory – adorned with a wreath by the local Morris side, the Broadwood Men, in a ceremony held every Mayday*

HORSHAM FOLK

MARKET TOWN MUSIC

Probably because of the presence of the Broadwoods in the area, most of the traditional Sussex music collected in the early days of the folk revival came from around Horsham. No doubt there was just as much going on elsewhere in the county – W. Percy Merrick did track down a few tunes from Henry Hills (*c. 1831-1901*) down the road in Lodsworth, near Petworth – but it was the singers and players of Horsham who attracted the most attention.

The real giant of the time was Henry Burstow (*1826-1916*). A shoe-maker by trade, and a singer, bellringer and storyteller by inclination, Burstow had an encyclopedic knowledge of traditional songs and 'broad-side ballads', with a repertoire of over 400 tunes. He met Lucy Broadwood in the 1890s, and she was immediately impressed with not only his memory but also his singing voice. Burstow gave her a list of the songs he knew and over the years she had him sing them to her, later publishing many of them in her book of *English Traditional Songs & Carols* in 1908. Not content with being immortalised in Broadwood's collection, and needing a spot of cash to help in his later years, Burstow also wrote the wonderfully entertaining *Reminiscences of Horsham*, published in 1911, 'being the Recollections of Henry Burstow The Celebrated Bellringer and Songsinger... together with a list of the 400 and odd Songs he sings from memory'.

It was Henry's singing, recommended by Broadwood, that brought Ralph Vaughan Williams back to Sussex in the early years of the 20th century, but he discovered more than Burstow in Horsham. In Monk's Gate, a few miles south of the town, he came across Harriet Verrall, who sang him several of the songs she had grown up with. She provided a couple of the best known Sussex tunes arranged by Vaughan Williams: the *Sussex Carol* ('On Christmas night all Christians sing'), and the

[16]

traditional melody for 'Welcome Sailor' (and also for 'The Blacksmith'), now better known as the tune for Bunyan's 'He who would valiant be' and dubbed *Monk's Gate* by its collector. He also wrote a *Fantasia on Sussex Folk Tunes*, no doubt inspired by his visits to Horsham.

Traditional music in Sussex was not confined to singing: most villages had a band to accompany their dances, which often played in church too. In Warnham, just north of Horsham, the band was led by Michael Turner (*1796-1885*), fiddler. Like Burstow, Turner was a cobbler and bellringer, and played at Burstow's wedding, so the two men more than likely shared some music too, but the instrumental music was not considered 'traditional' enough to figure in the Broadwoods' collections.

Horsham was at the forefront of the later folk revival of the 1960s too, thanks largely to the efforts of musician and writer Tony Wales (*1925-2007*). As far back as 1953, he started the first folk club in Sussex, the Horsham Songswappers, later becoming the Horsham Folk Club which is still meeting regularly, and in 1957 recorded the first album of traditional Sussex songs with his friend Peter Baxter on guitar. Throughout his career, Tony wrote more than 40 books on Sussex folk music and customs, and even a guide to the dialect, but still found time to run his barn dance band, the Derrydowners.

The Halls of Horsham

There's a nice feeling of continuity about folk music in Horsham, epitomised by the story of the Hall family. Mabs Hall and her son Gordon only started singing in public in the 1980s, encouraged by Bob Copper. Mabs, born in 1900 in Wivelsfield to a musical family, married and moved to London after World War I. Gordon was born there in 1932, and the family moved to Leeds and later Swansea, but returned to Sussex in 1939, settling first in 34 The Bishopric, Horsham – which by delightful coincidence had once been the home of Henry Burstow.

Top Places
- ⟩ *Monk's Gate, home of Harriet Verrall*
- ⟩ *Warnham, home of Michael Turner*

Top Read
- ⟩ *Henry Burstow's Reminiscences of Horsham*

MEET THE COPPERS

THE COPPER FAMILY

W hat Henry Burstow did for Sussex music in the first folk song revival, the Copper family did in the subsequent one. And where the focus had been on Horsham and West Sussex, from the 1950s attention was drawn eastwards across the county to the Coppers' home village of Rottingdean.

In fact, the Coppers had not been overlooked by the early folk song collectors; the family had been well known locally as singers of unaccompanied songs since the beginning of the 19th century, and were 'discovered' by Kate Lee in 1898. Lee, although one of the founders of the Folk Song Society, unfortunately did not have as high a profile as Lucy Broadwood or Vaughan Williams, so her discovery was somewhat overshadowed, and remained relatively neglected, except by the cognoscenti, for another 50 years.

The two singers she came across were James 'Brasser' Copper (*1845-1924*), who worked on the farms of the village squire, and his brother Thomas (*c.1847-c.1936*), the landlord of the local pub, the Black Horse – which incidentally is still to be found on Rottingdean High Street, and not that much changed since Thomas's day. The brothers were called up to the 'big house' of Sir Edward Carson QC where Lee was visiting. More used to singing at home with the family, or in Thomas's inn, they suddenly found themselves minor celebrities; Lee was inspired to set up the Folk Song Society, and made the brothers honorary founder members, but this went largely unnoticed – certainly in Rottingdean.

Nevertheless, their brief stardom brought them some recognition, and ensured that what had hitherto been an oral tradition was being written down. James in particular made a point of writing out the words to his songs with his idiosyncratic spellings, and encouraging the family (and indeed the whole village) to carry on the old traditions.

This they did with enthusiasm. Brasser (as his grandson Bob remarked once, you don't need a degree in metallurgy to work out how he got the nickname) had two sons, John (*c.1879-1952*) and Jim (*1882-1954*) who eagerly followed in their father's (and uncle's) footsteps, and did so for the love of singing rather than any chance of fame, as by the turn of the century they were pretty much forgotten by anybody outside Rottingdean. John was a shepherd and Jim a carter who went on to take over as Bailiff of the farms after his father retired, so music-making was very much an amateur occupation for the family. With four powerful Copper voices the harmonised singing in the 'Black Un' became a Saturday night attraction, earning them much-appreciated free beers as well as a strong local following.

And so it went on, through World War I and into the 1920s, with the next generation joining in. But between the two world wars, the area around Rottingdean began to change rapidly: the farms were in decline, and land was being sold off for housing. Farm workers like Jim Copper had to find alternative work – he became a blacksmith and carpenter, but his brother John remained a shepherd – and the old ways were disappearing. Except in one respect: the family remained in close contact, taking every opportunity for a sing, and Jim was determined the tradition shouldn't peter out. He, like his father had done before, wrote down nearly a hundred of the family songs in a book dedicated to his children, Topsy (Frances Joyce) and Trooper (Bob), in 1936.

Brasser died in 1924, but was to be succeeded by his grandchildren: John's son Walter Ronald, known as Ron (*c.1913-79*), and Jim's son Bob (*1915-2004*). Interest in folk song was by then on the wane with the rise in popularity of the gramophone and wireless and, apart from in some small rural pockets of the county such as Rottingdean, the old songs were not being performed anywhere. Undeterred, the Coppers continued to carry the torch, with the quartet of Jim, John, Ron and Bob still meeting regularly to sing together – but more for their own satisfaction than for an audience. Bob had by then joined the police and moved to West Sussex, but made regular trips back to complete the quartet. Even World War II failed to break up the musical partnership.

Until, not long after World War II, they came to the attention of the BBC thanks to Jim's bloody-minded outspokenness.

The singing family could have gone on, unnoticed by the outside world, if it hadn't been for a chance remark by Jim, visiting Bob in Peacehaven in 1950. He'd heard one of the songs they used to sing on the wireless, probably in a highly sanitised version, and was understandably annoyed. He told Bob that they 'didn't make much of a job of it' and 'didn't know the right words for a start', so Bob suggested that he didn't just complain to the BBC, but also tell them they had plenty more songs like it.

Jim duly wrote his complaint, and received a telegram from the BBC telling him that a reporter was on his way to meet the Coppers. What followed was one of the defining moments of the coming folk revival. The Home Service featured Jim and Bob in a episode of *Country Magazine*, and the following year broadcast *The Life of James Copper*, honouring him with a front cover photo on the *Radio Times*. This was followed by an invitation for Jim, Bob, John and Ron to sing at the Royal Albert Hall as part of the Festival of Britain, then television appearances, and the Copper family became nationally known.

John died shortly after the Albert Hall concert, but yet another generation was to ready take his place: Bob's son John and daughter Jill joined in, and they appeared together to record the iconic four-LP boxed set *A Song for Every Season* (now a real collectors' piece) in 1971. And when Ron died, in 1979, Jill's husband Jon Barratt was brought into the fold, later to be followed by Bob's grandchildren.

The core repertoire remained much the same, though: the traditional songs that had been passed down through the generations. The group was also still very much a family affair. The only thing that had changed was the audience – it had grown from the regulars in the taproom at the Black Horse to nationwide appreciation, and even international recognition. Bob was particularly in the limelight, writing books about the family, the songs, and Sussex life, and broadcasting regularly. He was awarded an honorary MA by the University of Sussex in 2000, and an MBE only days before he died in 2004.

As ever, the family goes on singing. As well as the Copper Family, the younger generation have formed their own group, The Young Coppers, consisting of Bob's six grandchildren: Mark, Andy and Sean Barratt, and Ben, Lucy and Tom Copper. Folk music may go in and out of fashion, but there's no sign of the Coppers ever giving up on their family tradition.

Top Place
- *The Black Horse, High Street, Rottingdean*

Top Reads
BOB COPPER'S BOOKS
- *A Song for Every Season: A Hundred Years of a Sussex Farming Family (London: Heinemann, 1971)*
- *Early to Rise: A Sussex Boyhood (London: Heinemann, 1976)*
- *Bob Copper's Sussex (SB Publications, 1997)*
- *Across Sussex with Belloc: In the Footsteps of the Four Men (Sutton Publishing, 1995)*

Top Anthologies
- *Songs and Southern Breezes: Country Folk and Country Ways (Heinemann, 1973)*
- *The Copper Family Song Book (Coppersongs, 1995)*

Top Tunes
- *Select Discography: A Song for Every Season*
- *Coppersongs: A Living Tradition*
- *Coppersongs 2*
- *Coppersongs 3: The Legacy Continues*
- *The Banks of Claudy*
- *Twankydillo*
- *Come Write Me Down*
- *See www.thecopperfamily.com for full details of all books and records*

SUSSEX SONGSHEET

LOCAL FOLK SONGS

This small selection of traditional songs from Sussex encapsulates some of the perennial themes found in local folk song: the first is a typical rural ballad, featuring the simple shepherd and his love; the second is the inevitable drinking song; and finally, a whimsical ditty, including lines that capture the humour of 'silly Sussex'.

SHEPHERD OF THE DOWNS

A shepherd of the downs being weary
    of his port
Retired to the hills where he used
    to resort.
In want of refreshment he laid himself
    down,
He wanted no riches, nor wealth from
    the Crown.

He drank of the cold brook, he ate of
    the tree,
Himself he did enjoy from all sorrow
    was free,
He valued no girl be she ever so fair,
No pride nor ambition he valued
    no care.

As he was a-walking one evening
    so clear
A heavenly sweet voice sounded soft in
    his ear.
He stood like a post not one step could
    he move,
He knew not what hailed him but
    thought it was love.

He beheld a young damsel, a fair
    modest bride
She had something amiss and
    disguised in her face.
Disguised in her face she unto him
    did say,
How now, Master Shepherd, how came
    you this way?

The shepherd he replied and modestly
    said,
I never was surprised before at a maid.
When first you beheld me from sorrow
    I was free,
But now you have stolen my poor
    heart from me.

He took her by the hand and thus he
    did say
We will get married pretty Betsy
    today.
So to church they did go and were
    married we hear,
And now he'll enjoy pretty Betsy
    his dear.

TWANKYDILLO

Here's a health to the jolly black-
    smith the best of all fellows
Who works at his anvil while the
    boy blows the bellows,
Which makes his bright hammer to
    rise and to fall.
There's the old Cole and the young
    Cole and the old Cole of all,
Twanky dillo, twanky dillo, twanky
    dillo, dillo, dillo, dillo,
And the roaring pair of bagpipes
    made from the green willow.

If a gentleman calls with his horse
    to be shoed
He will make no denial to one pot
    or two
Which makes his bright hammer to
    rise and to fall etc.

Here's a health to that pretty girl
    the one I love best
Who kindles her fire all in her own
    breast,
Which makes his bright hammer to
    rise and to fall etc.

Here's a health to our King and
    likewise our Queen
And to all the Royal Family
    wherever they're seen,
Which makes his bright hammer to
    rise and to fall etc.
Green willow, green willow, green
    willow, willow, willow,
And the roaring pair of bagpipes
    made from the green willow.

TWO OLD CROWS

There was a crow sat on a tree
And he was as black as black
    could be.

Now this old crow said to his mate,
Let us go and find something
    to eat.

They flew across the wide, wild
    plain,
To where a farmer had sown some
    grain.

Up came the farmer with his gun,
And he shot them both excepting
    one.

The one that escaped flew back to
    the tree
And he said, You old farmer you
    can't shoot me.

THE SUSSEX REVIVAL

SUSSEX FOLK MUSIC, OLD & NEW

It's in the nature of folk music that most of its practitioners remain unsung heroes. Until the collectors came along, folk musicians had only a very local following, and before recording technology, the tunes were passed down orally through the generations. A few achieved some fame thanks to the revival of interest in traditional music, but there have been just as many (if not more) who have eluded public attention. And let's not forget that the vast majority of them, until the 1960s folk revival, were not professional – their music was what they did for fun.

Nevertheless, there have been a handful whose talents attracted a wider audience, for one reason or another. Michael Blann (*1843-1934*), for instance, the shepherd from Upper Beeding who wrote down the words to the songs he knew in a notebook which is now in Worthing Museum. Or the various singers tracked down by Bob Copper in the 1950s: George Attrill, the road worker from Stopham, near Pulborough; the Hastings fisherman Noah Gillette; and the songbook left by John Johnson of Fittleworth. Folk song enthusiasts also acted as a springboard for characters such as George Townshend of East Chiltington, near Lewes, Johnny Doughty, originally from Brighton and later in Rye, and Bob Lewis, whose stamping ground was around Midhurst. Others, like George 'Pop' Maynard in Copthorne and George 'Spike' Spicer in Selsfield, attracted a following from beyond their native Sussex.

One or two gained their fame simply because of their outstanding performances. Lewis Tester (*1886-1972*), known to everyone as 'Scan' (short for 'scantelope', a family nickname whose origins are lost in the mists of time) progressed from playing his concertina, melodeon, bandoneon and fiddle in the pubs of Chelwood Gate and Horsted Keynes to concerts at the Royal Festival Hall. He and his brothers Will and Trayton formed a country dance band (he called it a 'jazz band') Tester's

Imperial to play at local dances and weddings, and travelled to Kent to entertain the gypsies during the hop-picking season. When he came to the notice of Reg Hall, who ran a folk club in Islington, he brought the old Sussex music to London, and recorded fifty-odd tunes on the album *I Never Played To Many Posh Dances* (sometimes misquoted as '*I Never Played Too Many Posh Dances*'). Interestingly, Reg Hall maintained his links with the county, becoming a research fellow and gaining his doctorate at the University of Sussex.

The explosion of interest in folk that started with the broadcasts of the Copper Family threw the spotlight on to Sussex. Foremost among the evangelists of Sussex folk was Hastings-born Shirley Collins (*born 1935*). Prompted by a love affair with the exiled American folk collector Alan Lomax, she returned to singing the praises of English traditional music, notably in the 1967 album of mainly Sussex tunes *The Sweet Primeroses*, accompanied by her sister Dolly (*1933-95*). This was followed by several groundbreaking recordings, reinvigorating the old songs with new instrumentation and, in 1971, with her husband and former founding member of the 'folk-rock' bands Fairport Convention and Steeleye Span, Ashley Hutchings, formed the Etchingham Steam Band, along with Terry Potter, Ian Holder and Vic Gammon. Spin-off bands such as the Albion Dance Band extended the range of this all-acoustic group to include electric and medieval instruments.

Hastings Folk

After Hutchings left Steeleye Span, they continued their Sussex connections when fiddler Peter Knight joined the line-up, and later with the inclusion of rock and jazz drummer Liam Genockey (see *pp.70-71*) – both residents of Hastings. Several other 'furriners' have also been tempted to move to the town by its lively folk music scene, including the late Dave Roberts of Blowzabella, and fiddler Barry Dransfield.

Top Tunes
- *Various artists, Just Another Saturday Night: Sussex 1960 (MT CD 309-10)*
- SCAN TESTER, *I Never Played to Many Posh Dances*
- SHIRLEY COLLINS, *The Sweet Primeroses*
- THE ETCHINGHAM STEAM BAND, *The Etchingham Steam Band*

MEET THE FOLK

THE SUSSEX FOLK SCENE

The heyday of the folk revival may be long gone, but there's still a thriving folk scene in Sussex. In the time-honoured tradition, a lot of the music happens in pubs scattered across the county, either spontaneously or on regular folk nights, and these venues tend to have a strong local following. Sadly, the enthusiasts are in the main middle-aged (and middle-class), and the local venues are not attracting the generation brought up on a diet of rock and pop, so unless there's an injection of new life into the genre on the lines of the 'folk-rock' revolution, it faces yet another decline in popularity.

But let's not anticipate the seemingly inevitable doom; there's plenty to enjoy still, and something for all tastes. As well as the informal pub sessions, there are a number of folk clubs that meet regularly – notably the Horsham Folk Club set up by Tony Wales in the 1950s and still going strong at the Normandy Centre, Denne Road on Sunday nights, the Footlights at the Village Hall in West Chiltington, and the Willows Folk Club at the Pavilion of Arundel Cricket Club. Other well-established clubs in West Sussex are based in pubs, which on other nights of the week may play host to less traditional music – a trend which has seen some folk clubs squeezed out of existence or forced to find alternative venues. Among the healthy survivors are the Chichester Folk Song Club, which meets at The 4 Chesnuts (*sic*) in Oving Road, and the Washington Music Club at the Frankland Arms.

If anything, folk clubs seem to be doing even better in the eastern half of the county: Lewes boasts at least two with the Lewes Arms Folk Club in Mount Place, and folk nights every Thursday down the road in The Royal Oak, Station Street, run by Vic and Tina Smith of the Sussex Pistols. Other clubs that still attract a large following include the one at The Lamb in High Street, Eastbourne, and the Seaford Folk and Song

Club, now back at their home in the Wellington, after being exiled to the Beachcomber by the encroaching pub restaurant business. For those who prefer a more rustic setting, the White Horse Folk Club in Bodle Street Green and the Six Bells Folk and Blues Club at Chiddingly provide suitably rural surroundings, and the latter has an annual mini-festival.

Of the many clubs to have sprung up in the major towns during the 1960s little has survived, save the Brighton Folk Club at the Hobgoblin in London Road and the Brighton Singers' Club (at various venues), although a sporadic impromptu folk scene continues in several urban pubs. (See Clive Bennett's book *Sussex Folk* for a history of the folk song revival in Sussex and the clubs it spawned.)

The really optimistic signs, however, are the folk festivals across the county. Although we no longer have the Horsham Festival, which ran throughout the 1960s, some later gatherings have proved enormously succesful. The annual Crawley Folk Festival seems to go from strength to strength, and the Eastbourne Lammas Festival has now established itself as a major event since its small beginnings in 2001. Also worthy of mention is the Lewes Folk Rock Festival, filling a gap in the market, and the Black Horse Festival at Telham, which devotes one of its three days to folk and acoustic music.

Sussex dance

One area of the folk tradition that remains perennially popular in Sussex is dancing. Morris sides abound all over the county, and the Mayday festival of Jack in the Green in Hastings brings dancers from all over Britain (and even beyond) for a non-stop weekend of celebration, surreally coinciding with the annual pilgrimage of bikers to the town. For more serious dance enthusiasts, Eastbourne hosts an International Folkdance Festival in May.

Top Places
- The 4 Chesnuts, *Oving Road, Chichester*
- The Frankland Arms, *Washington*
- The Six Bells, *Chiddingly*
- The White Horse, *Bodle Street Green*

PART TWO

CLASSICAL SUSSEX

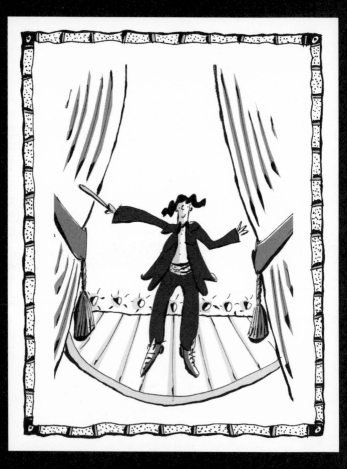

Classical music has played an important part in British culture, but the contribution of English composers has not always been consistent. After the 'Golden Age' of the Elizabethan madrigalists, musical fashion was dictated from mainland Europe, and only a handful of English composers stood out – notably Henry Purcell in the 17th century, followed by George Frideric Handel, a German, writing in a predominantly Italian style, but living in England. Even the revival of English music in Victorian times was led by another German, Felix Mendelssohn, and it wasn't until the late 19th century that any great English composers emerged.

Of course, most of this musical activity was centred in London, so you'd expect provincial Sussex not to figure very prominently in the musical history books. Which, actually, it doesn't, at least until very recently but this is more the fault of musicologists than any lack of home-grown talent. The fact that many leading musicians have their roots in the county or have chosen to live here is often overlooked and the contribution Sussex has made is seldom mentioned.

Several composers are more famous for their associations with other places: Edward Elgar with the Malverns, for instance, or Ralph Vaughan Williams with Gloucestershire, and even Claude Debussy with his native France, but all have been inspired at one time or another by their stays in Sussex, as we shall see. Some, like Thomas Weelkes, the scurrilous Elizabethen madrigalist, were born and spent most of their lives here. Others, such as John Ireland and Frank Bridge, made their homes here because they found inspiration in the Sussex countryside. Havergal Brian, Arnold Bax and John Tavener came to Sussex as a retreat from city life, and one or two, notably the eccentric Percy Grainger, have ended up in Sussex by chance. Unlikely as it might seem in sleepy Sussex, some have been attracted to the county by the opportunity to work in an internationally recognised centre of new music, the University of Sussex, including leading contemporary composers Jonathan Harvey and Michael Finnissy.

THOMAS WEELKES

THE GREAT ELIZABETHAN

Arguably the finest composer Sussex has ever produced, Thomas Weelkes was born in Elsted c.1576 (he was baptised on 25th October 1576) and died in London c.30th November 1623 (buried 1st December 1623). Weelkes wrote several volumes of madrigals, a large catalogue of church music and some pieces for instrumental consort which have earned him the reputation as one of the outstanding musicians of the Elizabethan and Jacobean era. Unfortunately, in his own lifetime he gained an altogether different reputation as well – as an unreliable, foul-mouthed drunkard.

Not much is known of Weelkes's early life, save that he was born in Elsted, a small village between Midhurst and Petersfield. He was quite probably the son of the Elsted rector, John Weeke (it seems that spelling wasn't a strong point in the family – subsequent generations have adopted the names Wilkes, Weekes and Weeks, too, although I can trace no relation), and was baptised on 25th October 1576, presumably by his father, so we can assume that he first saw the light of day in that year or not very long before. He apparently started his musical education in 1586, discovering a natural talent for composition, leading to the publication in 1597 of his first collection of madrigals.

Unlike his contemporaries, he did not seek a court appointment in London to pursue his musical ambitions; instead, during his teens he worked locally (probably as a court musician) for a couple of lesser noblemen, George Phillpot and Edward Darcye until 1598, when he was appointed organist of Winchester College. During the three or four years he was at the College, he wrote a further two books of madrigals, and contributed 'As Vesta was, from Latmos Hill Descending' to an anthology of madrigals, *The Triumphes of Oriana*, compiled by Thomas Morley in honour of Queen Elizabeth I. Although Weelkes produced some of his finest work in Winchester, he was not comfortable with the academic atmosphere at the College, as he felt that his only talent was for music.

So, some time in 1602, he moved to Chichester and took up a post as choirmaster and organist in the Cathedral – and at a much higher salary than he was getting at Winchester (£15 2s 4d a year, as opposed to 13s 4d a quarter; quite a substantial pay rise); and he landed a nice little side line as a lay clerk with Bishop Sherborne's foundation too. At about this time he was also awarded a BMus degree from New College, Oxford, and seemed to be getting the recognition he deserved. In Chichester he met and married the daughter of a local merchant, Elizabeth Sandham, and all appeared to be going well for him. Which, for a few years anyway, it did. He and his wife produced a family (at least three children), and he turned his hand to composing church music for the Cathedral, as well as a third volume of madrigals, *Ayeres or Phantastick Spirites for Three Voices*. But it wasn't to last. Weelkes's appetite for strong liquor didn't go unnoticed, and could only be overlooked for so long...

Works to listen for

Weelkes's madrigals frequently crop up in recordings and performances by choral groups: the best known and most usually heard are, as you would expect, his best works, including 'As Vesta was, from Latmos Hill Descending', the rousing 'Strike it up Tabor' and 'Come Sirrah Jacke Hoe', and the extraordinarily expressive 'O Care Thou Wilt Dispatch Mee' and 'Thule, the Period of Cosmographie'. And if you get the chance, don't miss his sacred anthems and services – especially if performed in Chichester Cathedral.

Musicians in the time of Weelkes, as today, were not renowned for their moderate behaviour, and a certain amount of unruliness and insubordination was almost expected of them by their employers. The royal courts, and even the churches, had to put up with bad timekeeping, occasional absences due to overindulgence, and a certain amount of horseplay from the musicians, and more often than not punished them only with a caution or at worst a small fine. Weelkes however pushed his luck with the authorities at Chichester Cathedral.

As early as 1609 he was in trouble for going 'absent without leave' on more than one occasion, and word was getting around that he was rather too fond of frequent trips to the ale house. As well as making him unreliable as a choirmaster and organist, the drink brought out the worst in him too: he was known by all locally as 'a comon drunckard and notorious swearer & blasphemer' – not ideal qualities in an employee of the church. Within a few years, he had incurred the wrath of the cathedral authorities, and was reprimanded several times, and had even been arrested for being drunk and disorderly in public.

Despite being given plenty of time to reform his ways, he continued to drink and misbehave until the situation became intolerable for his employers. There is an apocryphal story that during one of his drinking bouts he urinated on the Dean from the organ loft, which, if true, must have been the last straw. The bishop was forced to dismiss him from the post of organist and Informator Choristarum in 1617 (although he kept the well-paid post of Sherborne clerk), in the hope that this would bring him to his senses.

Apparently not. The carousing and cursing went on unabated, even in cathedral services, and he did

> dyvers times & very often come so disguised eyther from the Taverne or Ale house
> into the quire as is muche to be lamented' [and did] 'bothe curse & sweare
> most dreadfully ... though he hath bene often tymes admonished... he daylye
> continue the same, & is rather worse than better;

but it seems the bishop relented – Weelkes's musical talent was presumably missed in the choir, even if his behaviour wasn't – and gave him his old job back.

He spent the last few years of his life ostensibly at Chichester Cathedral, but in fact only carrying out his duties there rather sporadically, spending much of his time in London, especially after the death of his wife in 1622.

Weelkes died on either 30th November or 1st December 1623 at the age of 47, while staying with a friend, ironically enough named Henry Drinkwater.

The Mysterious Turges (or Sturges) family

Edmund Turges (*born c.1450, died on an unknown date*) is known today for the few extant choral pieces he wrote, included in the Eton Choirbook and the Fayrfax Book of c.1500, and the Caius Choirbook of c.1520. Sometimes erroneously referred to as 'Sturges', or perhaps unsurprisingly confused with a completely different composer called Edmund Sturges, he is possibly (but only possibly, no records have survived) a member of the musical family of Turges from Petworth. Another Edmund Turges (*born 1506*), and William Turges (perhaps grandsons of the original Turges) went to King's College, Cambridge, while a further William, George and James all held musical posts at Arundel College in the early 16th century.

Chichester Psalms

Leonard Bernstein (*1918-1990*) was commissioned to write a choral work for the 1965 Southern Cathedrals' Festival by the Dean and organist of Chichester Cathedral. The resulting setting of psalms from the Hebrew Bible, *Chichester Psalms* for boy treble (or countertenor), solo vocal quartet, choir and orchestra had its UK premiere at the Cathedral in July that year, a few months after its first performance in Philharmonic Hall, New York.

Gustav Holst

Weelkes isn't the only musician to be commemorated in Chichester Cathedral. A few feet away from his memorial stone lie the ashes of Gustav Holst (*1874-1934*), the composer of *The Planets* suite, and elsewhere there is a memorial to the music-hall singer and comedian Chesney Allen, who died in nearby Midhurst, and whose ashes are also interred in the cathedral.

Top Place
- *Chichester Cathedral, memorial stones of Weelkes, Holst and Allen*

Top Tunes
- *As Vesta was, from Latmos Hill Descending*
- *Strike it up Tabor*
- *O Care Thou Wilt Dispatch Mee*

VAUGHAN WILLIAMS & BAX

ESTABLISHMENT COMPOSERS

Sussex had to wait a long time after Weelkes before a maj[or] composer was to emerge – but there's no shame in that, as so [did] the rest of England; other than Purcell, there was no home-grow[n] talent to speak of between the 'golden age' of Elizabethan music and [the] late 19th century. When at last England struggled out of the musi[cal] doldrums, a good number of the finest composers had links to the coun[ty] which are sadly often overlooked.

One such musician was Ralph Vaughan Williams (*1872-1958*). Mu[ch] is made of the fact he was born in Down Ampney, Gloucestershire, b[ut] he actually only lived there for two and a half years: when his father di[ed] suddenly in 1875, the family moved to his mother's family home, Le[ith] Hill Place, near Dorking in Surrey. In 1883, young Ralph was sent [to] Field House preparatory school in Rottingdean (still in existence tod[ay] as St Aubyn's School), before going on to Charterhouse School in 18[ ] and then on to Cambridge. His stay at Field House was the first [of] several associations with Sussex.

During his studies at Cambridge, Vaughan Williams came in[to] contact with some of the great liberal thinkers of the time, and throu[gh] them met Adeline Fisher, daughter of the historian and politician Herb[ert] Fisher, a cousin of Virginia Woolf and Vanessa Bell. Ralph and Adeli[ne] were married at All Saints Church in Hove in October 1897, and sp[ent] their honeymoon in Berlin, where Vaughan Williams studied with M[ax] Bruch. When they returned, he caught the folk song-collecting bug th[at] was infecting the music scene of the time, and around the turn of t[he] century collaborated with Lucy Broadwood (*see pp. 14-15*), bringing h[im] back to Sussex once more.

Where Vaughan Williams spent some of his early life in Sussex, Arn[old] Bax (*1883-1953*) did the more predictable thing and retired to the coun[ty]

Throughout his creative life, he had had an uneasy relationship with the musical establishment: he was given a knighthood in 1937 in recognition of his achievements, and made Master of the King's Music in 1942, but was never completely comfortable with these honours. Much of his time had been spent travelling through Scandinavia, Russia and Ukraine, and settling for a while in Ireland, and his music reflected his fascination with these exotic cultures. He felt alienated from the mainstream of English music, despite his previous successes, and was increasingly thought of as rather old-fashioned. Depression and alcoholism set in, and he wrote little of any importance after 1940, preferring to withdraw into the Sussex countryside, where he spent his final years living in the White Horse Hotel at Storrington. Perhaps happily for him, he died in Cork during one of the regular trips he made to Ireland.

His successor as Master of the Queen's music 1953-75, Sir Arthur Bliss, has been claimed by Brighton as a one-time resident, but there seems to be no foundation for this – certainly his family have no knowledge of his having lived there. As far as we know, his only connection with Sussex was as President of the Hove Gramophone Society, and (on the strength of his having written the ballet *Checkmate*) coming down to open the Hastings International Chess Congress in the 1960s.

Field House & the White Horse

Vaughan Williams's old school can still be found on the High Street in Rottingdean. It started life in the 1820s as part of the school at The Grange run by Dr Hooker, and was known as Field House until it was refounded in 1895 as St Aubyn's School.

The White Horse at Storrington these days trades more on its 400-year reputation as a coaching inn than as the retirement home of Sir Arnold Bax, but is nevertheless worth a visit. If funds permit, there are plans to commemorate Bax jointly with John Ireland (see p.36) in a museum in the South Downs National Park.

Top Tunes
- VAUGHAN WILLIAMS, *The Lark Ascending; The Sussex Carol; Fantasia on Sussex Folk Tunes*
- BAX, *The seven Symphonies; music for the films Malta GC and Oliver Twist*

JOHN IRELAND

DOWNLAND INSPIRATION

P erhaps more than any other composer, John Ireland (*1879-1962*) found inspiration for his music in the Sussex countryside, particularly the Downland around Chanctonbury Ring. Born in Bowdon, near Altrincham, Manchester, Ireland studied at the Royal College of Music, becoming a teacher there himself, and only discovered Sussex when in his forties. On his first visit, he stayed in Ashington, and fell for the area in a big way. Over the next 30 years, he came down frequently to stay in Amberley, Ashington, Shipley, and Steyning, and nursed an ambition of one day living in the Rock Mill at Washington, a dream which he finally achieved in 1953.

But even before moving from London, much of his music had its origins in Sussex, either overtly as in the *Downland Suite*, *Amberley Wild Brooks*, or the *Legend for Piano and Orchestra* (referring to the legend of ghostly children from a leper colony to be seen on Harrow Hill), or more obliquely in his Piano Sonatas, and the Cello Sonata inspired by the 'Devil's Jumps' barrow cemetery. On his trips down here he would walk across the Downs, notebook in hand, and jot down ideas that he could take back to Chelsea to work on. He took his inspiration from the place itself rather than music associated with the area, developing a more 'continental' style influenced by Debussy and Ravel (and to some extent Stravinsky and Bartok), which is best described as 'English impressionism' – and which is perhaps the most appropriate style to capture the feel of the Sussex landscape. Because the impressionistic style he adopted is better suited to mainly small-scale works, such as his many piano pieces, songs and chamber works than symphonies and operas, Ireland composed comparatively little for orchestra, although some of his finest music is found in the Piano Concerto and the more popular *Downland Suite* (both inspired by his beloved Sussex).

He finally retired in 1953, when by happy coincidence Rock Mill came up for sale while he was holidaying in Ashington. Ireland seized the opportunity to settle in his adopted county. By this time he was quite frail, and he was looked after by his friend Norah Kirby. She remained in Sussex after his death in 1962, and for the next 20 years ran a small John Ireland museum in Steyning, unfortunately no longer there. Ireland is buried in Shipley churchyard, which has magnificent views across Chanctonbury Ring and the Downs he loved so much.

Rock Mill

The windmill at Rock, just to the west of the A24 and about 6 miles (10 km) north of Worthing, is still one of the most prominent man-made landmarks in the Washington area. The local council is hoping that it can be included in the South Downs National Park and made into a museum dedicated to Ireland and Arnold Bax, who lived not far away in Storrington.

A French impressionist in Eastbourne

Ireland was not the only impressionist composer to find inspiration in Sussex. Claude Debussy, usually thought of as archetypically French, wrote a couple of his best known pieces while staying at the Grand Hotel in Eastbourne in 1905: it is the English Channel, rather than la Manche, that is depicted in *La Mer*, and the *Reflets dans l'Eau* are those of the ornamental pond in Devonshire Park. But Debussy was not in Eastbourne through choice. He and his pregnant lover Emma Bardac (the future second Madame Debussy) were fleeing from France to avoid the scandal caused by their affair, leaving his wife Rosalie recovering from the gunshot wound of an unsuccessful suicide attempt.

Top Places
❯ Rock Mill, Washington, home of John Ireland
❯ The Grand Hotel, Eastbourne, where Debussy wrote La Mer

Top Tunes
❯ IRELAND, Downland Suite; Amberley Wild Brooks; Legend for Piano and Orchestra
❯ DEBUSSY, La Mer; Reflets dans l'Eau (from Images)

LAST NIGHT OF THE PROMS

LAND OF HOPE & GLORY

The two 'singalong' numbers that feature as the climax to the patriotic fervour of the *Last Night of the Proms*, Hubert Parry's setting of William Blake's *Jerusalem* and Edward Elgar's *Pomp and Circumstance March No. 1* ('Land of Hope and Glory'), may have become hackneyed by overexposure, but their popularity is deserved, as they are fine pieces by fine composers. What is less well known is that both Parry and Elgar found Sussex the ideal place to retreat from the pressures of musical life in London.

Sir Charles Hubert Hastings Parry (*1848-1918*) is only really remembered today as the composer of *Jerusalem*, but in his day he was recognised as a leading light in the so-called renaissance of English music. After studying at Oxford and Stuttgart, he moved to London, and taught at the Royal College of Music (RCM) from 1884. He was earning himself quite a reputation at the time with performances of his four symphonies, oratorios and operas, and he was appointed director of the RCM in 1894, and Professor of Music at Oxford University in 1900. Despite his undoubted success, he was never entirely comfortable with life in the city, and quite early in his career he commissioned Norman Shaw to design a house for him, which he had built in Sea Lane, Rustington, to the east of Littlehampton. From when Knights Croft House was finished, in 1879, Parry used it as a bolthole where he could relax and compose, and it was here that he was happiest. He retired from Oxford University in 1908, on doctor's orders (although he retained the directorship of RCM for the rest of his life), spending most of his time in Rustington in his final ten years. And it was in the music room of Knights Croft House at this time that he produced much of his best work, including the *Symphonic Fantasia*, the *Songs of Farewell* and *Jerusalem*. Not long after his death, his ghost was apparently seen wandering round the house, smiling.

Slightly younger than Parry, Sir Edward Elgar (*1857-1934*) came to prominence in the 1890s, securing his place in the musical history books with the Enigma Variations in 1899. By the outbreak of World War I, he was Britain's foremost composer but, like Parry, he was keen to find some respite from the hectic round of concerts and tours. Besides, his music was becoming less fashionable, except for the (in his opinion) inappropriately jingoistic adoption of 'Land of Hope and Glory' during the war, and he was finding it difficult to write music. His wife, Alice, found Brinkwells, a thatched cottage for rent in Fittleworth, between Pulborough and Petworth, and the couple moved there in May 1917. It was small but boasted a tennis court and a studio in the garden made partly from a railway carriage. Brinkwells gave him the impetus to compose again, and it was there that he wrote some of his finest chamber music, including the A minor Piano Quintet. When Alice died, in 1920, his plan was to buy the Fittleworth cottage for his retirement, but the landlord wasn't interested in selling. Elgar spent a further year in Brinkwells, during which time he completed his last great masterpiece, the Cello Concerto, before moving to Kempsey in Worcestershire.

Robert Walker

Brinkwells, Elgar's home in Fittleworth, was later occupied by the composer Robert Walker, founder of the Petworth Festival. Walker resurrected the notes that Elgar had made in 1913 for a piano concerto, and assembled them into a piece for piano and orchestra he called *Fragments of Elgar*, premiered by his pianist friend David Owen Norris (also from Fittleworth) in 1997.

Top Places
- ❂ *Knights Croft House, Sea Lane, Rustington, Hubert Parry's home*
- ❂ *Brinkwells, Fittleworth, Elgar's Sussex cottage*

Top Tunes
- ❂ PARRY, *Jerusalem*
- ❂ ELGAR, *Cello Concerto; Pomp and Circumstance March No. 1; Piano Quintet in A minor*

PERCY GRAINGER

OFFBEAT AVANT-GARDE

The eccentric and outrageous composer best known for arrangements of folk tunes such as *Country Gardens*, Per Grainger (*1882-1961*), was born in Brighton – the Brighton t is a suburb of Melbourne, Australia. His link to Sussex came much la in the suitably unlikely shape of a cottage in Pevensey Bay. His parents w both English immigrants and after they separated, his domineeri mother Rose (who had contracted syphilis from his alcoholic fath took him to Europe to study music. After some years in Frankfurt, moved to London with the ever-present Rose, and there struck u friendship with Edvard Grieg, who stirred up Grainger's interest collecting folk tunes. In the years up to the outbreak of World Wa he travelled around Britain recording rural folk songs and compos music which was an extraordinary mix of traditional tunes and ava garde experimentation.

Conservative Britain was no place for such an offbeat talent, so (and Rose) moved on again, this time to the United States. His less o landish music, particularly *Country Gardens*, proved popular there, earn him a reputation and enough money to buy a substantial property White Plains, New York, after the war. His relationship with mother was by then verging on the incestuous, and only prevented fr becoming so by her suicide in 1922.

Now that he was free of Rose's constant influence, he travelled wid collecting folk tunes in Scandinavia, and visiting Australia. On his way b to the United States in 1926, he met the Swedish-born artist and p Ella Viola Ström and, no doubt because of his obsession with Nor culture and the loss of his smothering mother, immediately fell in lo Unfortunately, Ström was returning to her home in England from a v to her fiancé. Undeterred, Grainger wooed her and visited her seve times at her cottage in Pevensey Bay, eventually persuading her to call off her engagement and marry him. Their wedding was classic Grainger showmanship: immediately after he had conducted the world premiere of the tone poem dedicated to his bride, *To A Nordic Princess*, they were married in the Hollywood Bowl with an audience of more than 20,000 adoring fans. The couple settled in White Plains, but kept the cottage in Sussex, which they used on and off until it was lent to Grainger's composer friend Cyril Scott just after World War II – but, other than a setting of the Sussex Mummers' Carol (which he got from Lucy Broadwood), traditional music from Sussex figures very little in his music.

Quite apart from his music, which was eccentric, Grainger courted controversy in other areas too: he was an outspoken white-aryan suprema-cist, maintaining that the Nordic, blue-eyed race was far superior to all others. Despite these views, which always just bordered on the racist and antisemitic, he was fascinated by folk music and instruments from all cultures, and was an admirer and close friend of Duke Ellington and George Gershwin. Another cause for raised eyebrows was his enthusi-astic participation in sado-masochism, which he made no effort to conceal – he even posed for photographs to illustrate his preferences.

Cyril Scott

While he was studying at the Hoch Conservatory in Frankfurt, Grainger fell in with a group of young English composers: Roger Quilter (see p.49), Henry Balfour Gardiner and Cyril Scott. Scott and Grainger remained friends after their return to England, and when Scott found himself practically destitute and with a failing marriage in 1945, Grainger immediately offered him (and his mistress) the cottage in Pevensey Bay. This was enough to get Scott back on his feet and a couple of years later he moved to Eastbourne, where he lived (with a lime-green piano and a neighbour's parrot) until his death in 1970.

Top Place
❯ *Pevensey Bay, home of Ella Viola Ström and Percy Grainger, and later Cyril Scott*

Top Tunes
❯ GRAINGER, *Country Gardens; To a Nordic Princess; Sussex Mummers' Carol*

FRANK BRIDGE

PEACEFUL REVOLUTIONARY

D escribed by his biographer, Rob Barnett, as a 'composer, courageous revolutionary and pacifist', Frank Bridge (*1879-1941*) is remembered today more for having taught Benjamin Britten than for his own music. This is a shame, as this Sussex-born musician was a fiercely independent composer who turned his back on the fashionable trends of his contemporaries to produce some of the most original British music of the early 20th century.

Bridge was born into a working-class family in Brighton; his father was a cordwainer (shoemaker), but also an enthusiastic amateur musician (later Musical Director of Brighton's Empire Theatre), who sent him to the local music school and encouraged him to go on to study violin and composition at the Royal College of Music. After graduating in 1904, Bridge switched from the violin to the viola and played with both the Joachim Quartet and the English String Quartet, at the same time having a reputation as a conductor – he was assistant to Thomas Beecham and deputised at the Promenade Concerts for Sir Henry Wood, who became a great champion of his work.

His compositions at this time were restricted mainly to chamber music and songs, as he was busy trying to earn a living by performing, but his first major orchestral pieces, the *Suite for Strings* (1910), *The Sea* (1911) and *Summer* (1914), with their mix of English pastoralism and Gallic impressionism brought him the public recognition he deserved. The advent of World War I, however, was to bring a change in his fortunes, and a profound change in his music.

As a committed pacifist, Bridge was deeply affected by the futility of World War I, which, coupled with lean times, virtually stopped his composing. After 1920, however, he started again with renewed vigour and a much more acerbic and modernistic style. With Marjorie Fass, Bridge and his wife Ethel, whom he had met at the Royal College of Music, bought land in Friston, between Eastbourne and Seaford, and had adjacent cottages built on the Downland there. The turning point came when he met Elizabeth Sprague Coolidge, the American millionaire and patron of the arts. Her patronage of Bridge's music brought him to American audiences and provided him with enough money to concentrate solely on his composition (although he did keep on one composition pupil, Benjamin Britten, who became almost an adopted son).

From his home at Friston Field, Bridge explored the expressionist techniques of Schoenberg and developed his own, rather more lyrical style, producing his undoubted masterpieces in the last two decades of his life: the Piano Sonata dedicated to the memory of composer Ernest Farrar, killed in action in France, *Enter Spring* (originally titled *On Friston Down*), *Oration for cello and orchestra*, *Phantasm for piano and orchestra*, the *Piano Trio No. 2*, the *Rebus Overture*, the *Violin Sonata No. 2*, and the third and fourth String Quartets.

Bridge's health deteriorated throughout the 1930s but he continued to compose. He was working on a symphony for strings when he died, in Eastbourne, in 1941.

Benjamin Britten

Benjamin Britten made frequent visits to Sussex to study with Bridge. He was only 15 when he started his lessons as Bridge's only pupil in 1928. From Bridge he learned not only the nuts and bolts of composition but was taken on walks and drives around the South Downs to learn to appreciate the beauty of the countryside, and at Friston was introduced to the latest ideas in all the other arts too. Above all, Bridge instilled in him his pacifist philosophy and aesthetics, which remained an important feature of Britten's work too. His debt to his teacher is honoured in the *Variations on a Theme of Frank Bridge* (1937), based on a theme from Bridge's *Three Idylls for String Quartet* (1906).

Top Place
❯ *Friston, home of Frank Bridge and much visited by Benjamin Britten*

Top Tunes
❯ BRIDGE, *The Sea; Enter Spring; The four String Quartets; Phantasm for piano and orchestra*

MUSICAL OPINION

THE CLASSICAL MUSIC MAGAZINE

There are many unsung heroes in the musical world: the conductors and soloists in orchestral concerts inevitably get more attention than the rank-and-file musicians of the band, and accompanists seldom get their share of the limelight. Often the glamour of the performers overshadows the brilliance of the composers, who only rarely appear to take their bows and, more often than not, only achieve star status posthumously. But there are others whose contribution to our enjoyment is barely noticed – the instrument makers and tuners, sound engineers, and all sorts of back-room boys (and girls) whose skills are essential to a successful performance. In classical music particularly, there are also publishers, editors and even librarians and music copyists, to ensure the performers are all reading from the same hymn sheet.

Then there are the music critics, often highly skilled musicians themselves, who help to inform audiences about performances and recordings through their columns in the newspapers or in specialist music periodicals. Which brings us back, at last but somehow inevitably, to Sussex; more specifically to St Leonards-on-Sea, where the venerable music journal *Musical Opinion* is now based. First published in 1877, it is the oldest classical music magazine in Britain, and has an enviable reputation for its reviews of concerts, recordings and books, but few of its readers realise it is not London-based. Denby Richards, the current editor, runs the entire operation from his home in St Leonards, and the editorial and production team (even the printers) are based in Hastings and St Leonards. Its sister publication, *The Organ*, was launched in 1921, and is as highly regarded in its field – and has a St Leonards connection too: from 1993 to 2007 it was under the editorship of Brian Hick, from his home less than a mile away from Musical Opinion's headquarters.

Another music journalist, amongst many other things, was Gerald Abraham (*1904-1988*), who lived at Ebernoe, near Petworth. As a young man he was Assistant Editor at the *Radio Times* and Deputy Editor of *The Listener*, moving on to become Director of the Gramophone Department of the BBC and one of the driving forces behind the formation of the Third Programme (now Radio 3) in 1946, and eventually becoming Assistant Controller of Music at the BBC after a period as Professor of Music at Liverpool University. He is, however, better known – in so far as any musicologist is well known – for his writings on music, either as music critic of the *Daily Telegraph*, or the author of many books and articles on classical music. His particular interest was in Russian and Soviet composers, which he wrote about with scholarly precision for students of the subject, but he also had a wide and perceptive knowledge of music history from medieval to modern times, which he made accessible to a wider public through *The Concise Oxford History of Music* and his contribution to the *New Oxford History of Music*, and as editor of the very readable *Music of the Masters* series. Not bad going for an almost completely self-taught musician.

Amati Publishing

Even further removed from musical performance, but no less valuable in terms of maintaining standards of excellence, are the publishers of information on musical instruments. The standard work on violins, for instance, which is on the shelves of every self-respecting luthier or dealer, is *William Henley's Universal Dictionary of Violin and Bow Makers*, a labour of love completed by Cyril Woodcock after the author's death in 1957 and published by the very specialist Amati Publishing of Brighton. The supplement to this mighty tome, *Woodcock's Dictionary of Contemporary Violin and Bow Makers*, followed shortly after, again published by Amati.

Top Places
- St Leonards-on-Sea, notably the area designed by Decimus Burton known as Burton's St Leonards
- Ebernoe, Petworth, Gerald Abraham's home

MICHAEL TIPPETT

A CHILD OF OUR TIME

The Wadhurst Corps of the Salvation Army may be unknown to most concert-goers, but it does have a place in the musical history books. The corps's bandmaster in the 1950s, George Mallion, was a local fish and poultry monger, and among his customers was the composer Michael Tippett (*1905-1998*) who lived in nearby Tidebrook Manor. Every Christmas, the band went carolling around Wadhurst and tended to finish by playing outside Tippett's house, where they were then invited in for mince pies. One year Mallion asked if Tippett would consider writing something for the band and the resulting hymn tune, *Wadhurst* (for the words, 'Unto the hills around do I lift up my longing eyes'), was published in 1958. Perhaps it is not his best known or most significant piece but it was written at the time he was reaching the height of his compositional powers.

Tippett lived at Tidebrook, between Wadhurst and Mayfield, from 1951 to 1960, with his mother (who, among other quirks, put laxative in the food 'even when there were guests', according to Tippett's autobiography *Those Twentieth Century Blues*). From 1945 he had been Director of Music at Morley College, but in 1951 resigned in order to devote his time to composition, prompting the move to Sussex. He had already established his reputation as one of Britain's foremost composers by then, but, like Britten, was not entirely accepted by the musical establishment because of his pacifism (he was a conscientious objector during World War II, and was imprisoned for three months for not agreeing to the conditions of his registration), his left-wing politics and his homosexuality.

His period at Tidebrook gave him the opportunity to build on the successes of his early string quartets, the first Symphony and the oratorio *A Child of Our Time*, and saw the completion of his first opera,

Midsummer Marriage, in 1952. Further commissions followed: the *Fantasia Concertante on a Theme of Corelli*, a Concerto for Piano and Orchestra, a second Symphony, and the cantata *Crown of the Year*, along with many other smaller works, and in the final years of the 1950s the opera *King Priam*. All helped to secure Tippett's place as a major international composer.

The 1950s also saw him emerge as a lecturer and broadcaster, gathering his talks in the book *Moving into Aquarius* in 1958, and continuing his work with the Peace Pledge Union, which elected him their lifetime President in 1958. Tippett left Sussex in 1960 and later settled on the Marlborough Downs in Wiltshire. His musical achievements eventually received official recognition when he received a knighthood in the more liberal atmosphere of 1966, and the Order of Merit in 1988.

Gustav Holst

Although never a resident of Sussex (except posthumously – his ashes are buried in Chichester Cathedral), Gustav Holst (*1874-1934*) had strong links with the county through his friend Dr George Bell who, as Dean of Canterbury Cathedral, had commissioned him to write some music for the drama *The Coming of Christ*. Holst had some years earlier set up a series of Whitsuntide Festivals in Thaxted, Essex, and when Dr Bell was appointed Bishop of Chichester he suggested the festivals should be held at his Cathedral. Holst happily agreed and visited Bell many times to organise the events, always taking the opportunity to walk across the Downs to Midhurst and Pulborough, train and bus timetables in his pocket, before returning to London. The Whitsuntide Festivals successfully moved to their new home, and continued for some years there under Holst's directorship and later at Bosham and Boxgrove.

Top Places
- *Tidebrook Manor, Tippett's home in the 1950s*
- *Wadhurst, which gave its name to Tippett's hymn tune for the Salvation Army*
- *Chichester Cathedral, Holst's memorial stone*

Top Tunes
- THE OPERAS, *The Midsummer Marriage; King Priam*
  Fantasia Concertante on a Theme of Corelli; The four Symphonies

HAVERGAL BRIAN

PROLIFIC OBSCURITY

Famous more for his prolific output (including 32 symphon[ies] more than any other major composer since the time of Mo[zart] and Haydn) and the fact that his Symphony No. 1, 'The Goth[ic]' made it into the record books as the largest ever composed, than for [his] undoubted talent as a musician, Havergal Brian (*1876-1972*) [was] virtually ignored for much of his life, died in comparative obscurit[y in] Shoreham-by-Sea, and is still unjustly underrated.

Born into a working-class family in Dresden, Stoke-on-Trent, Will[iam] Brian (he took the name Havergal, in 1899, after a hymn-writing fam[ily]) started at a disadvantage in a predominantly middle-class musical wo[rld] and lacked the self-confidence to overcome his humble background. [He] married in 1898 and the couple had five children as he was strugglin[g to] get his music noticed, so lack of money also hampered his chances. [His] breakthrough came in 1907 when Henry Wood performed his *Eng[lish] Suite* at the London Promenade Concerts. Further performances [and] publication of his work followed, and his success seemed assure[d,] especially as a local businessman offered him an annual income of £[…] (a respectable salary then) to enable him to compose full-time.

It's possible that the patronage was counterproductive, howeve[r.] Brian left many of his musical projects unfinished, and adopted a rat[her] too lavish lifestyle. His marriage broke down in 1913 after an affair w[ith] a servant, Hilda Hayward, and much of his income went to his w[ife] while he set up home with Hilda. World War I further interrupted [his] musical activities, and the momentum was lost. He and Hilda move[d to] Birmingham after the war and then spent some years in Lewes [and] Brighton scratching a living by copying and arranging music and w[rit]-ing articles for musical journals. They eventually settled in Londo[n in] 1927, when he became Assistant Editor of *Musical Opinion* magazin[e.]

The regular income gave him the chance to resume his composing and to father another five children with Hilda, and finally to marry her once his first wife died in 1933. Compositions during this time included his symphonies and the opera *The Tigers*, based on his comically disastrous wartime experiences. But it wasn't until he was discovered by Robert Simpson, a BBC music producer, that any of his work was performed. Simpson persuaded Sir Adrian Boult to premiere the Eighth Symphony in 1954, arranged an amateur performance of the massive *Gothic Symphony* in 1961, and a professional premiere under Boult in 1966. Further lobbying on his behalf came from an unlikely source: Phil Lesh, bass guitarist of the psychedelic rock band the Grateful Dead, did much to promote later performances and recordings.

This public recognition would have been too late for most composers, but Brian was apparently made of sterner stuff. He 'retired' to Shoreham in 1958, aged 82, and immediately embarked on a decade of remarkable musical activity. From his home at No. 1 The Marlinspike, bought for him by his daughter Elfreda and her husband, he wrote his last 20 symphonies, bringing the total to a magnificent 32, and numerous other works in the next decade. He died after a fall in November 1972, without having heard the majority of his work performed, but knowing that the BBC had agreed to perform all of his symphonies.

Roger Quilter

Contemporary with Brian, Roger Quilter (*1877-1953*) could not have had a more different background and career. Born in Hove, Quilter was the son of a baronet, educated at Eton, and a student at the Hoch Conservatory with Percy Grainger and Cyril Scott. He wrote some light orchestral pieces which earned him an enthusiastic popularity, but is mainly remembered today for his more than one hundred songs, many of which are still regularly performed.

Top Place
❯ *No. 1 The Marlinspike, Shoreham-by-Sea, home of Havergal Brian*

Top Tunes
❯ BRIAN, *Symphony No. 1 'The Gothic'*
❯ QUILTER, *Songs: Love's Philosophy, Weep You No More; Children's Overture*

PROGRESSIVE v CONSERVATIVE

JOHN TAVERNER & JONATHAN HARVEY

Sussex has become home for two of Britain's leading contemporary composers: John Tavener (*born 1944*) and Jonathan Harvey (*born 1939*) both express their deeply felt religious and spiritual beliefs through their music, and both came to prominence in the musical maelstrom of the 1960s. There the similarities end, however – in fact, the two epitomise the polarised trends of classical music today, and point to a paradox in the worlds of the 'progressive' and 'conservative'.

John Tavener (not to be confused with the 16th-century composer John Taverner) came from a rather conventional Presbyterian family in Wembley Park, North London. His musical talent was apparent from an early age, and he won a scholarship to the Royal Academy of Music in 1962, originally intending to be a concert pianist, but devoting more and more time to his composition. Through the 1960s, he developed a deliberately iconoclastic style, incorporating elements of the latest ideas in modernist music. A performance by the newly-formed London Sinfonietta of his cantata *The Whale* perfectly captured the mood of London in the 'Swinging Sixties', and the flamboyantly dressed and long-haired Tavener was hailed as the new boy wonder of the classical music scene, and even made an impact on the pop scene too – John Lennon showed an interest in his music, and arranged for the Beatles' company, Apple, to record *The Whale*, *Celtic Requiem* and *Nomine Jesu*.

By this time, he had moved away from the austerity of Presbyterianism, preferring the dramatic ritual of the Roman Catholic church, and this was becoming increasingly apparent in his music, especially *Ultimos Ritos* (1972), in which his obsession with liturgical ritual underlies the structure of the music. But he was about to go through a spiritual crisis, eventually turning his back on Catholicism and joining the Russian Orthodox church in 1977. His spiritual journey was mirrored by the opera of the same time, *Thérèse*, and his adoption of early Byzantine scales in place of the dissonance of modernism marked his conversion.

Through the 1970s he gradually fell out of favour with the public and critics. He had dismissed Western culture as materialistic and lacking in spirituality, and in the 1980s he was writing almost exclusively church music – in a pared-down, almost minimalist style which had more in common with medieval plainchant and Eastern religious music than the 20th-century Western tradition. This simplicity and purity came from a belief that music should be composed intuitively, inspired by God, rather than by any cerebral or analytical process, and once again he captured the mood of the time: a public baffled by some of the excesses of the avant-garde found Tavener's sparse 'Orthodox' style refreshingly approachable. Starting with the short unaccompanied setting of Blake's *The Lamb* in 1985, Tavener became fashionable once more; pieces such as *The Protecting Veil* (premiered at the 1989 Proms) became surprising best-selling CDs, and his *Song for Athene* was sung at Princess Diana's funeral in 1997.

The 1990s saw not only his return to fame, but also some major changes in Tavener's life. His health had often been a problem (he has Marfan syndrome, and suffered a stroke at the age of 36) and after major heart surgery in 1991, moved from Wembley to a retreat in the Sussex Downs with his new wife Maryanna (they also acquired a house in his beloved Greece), where he continues to compose in an increasingly Eastern-inspired style. He was knighted in 2000.

Jonathan Harvey's career as a composer runs in parallel to Tavener's, but in an apparently different musical world. Born in 1939 in Sutton Coldfield, Harvey had a public school education at Repton, and won a scholarship to St John's College, Cambridge, where he gained a PhD, studying composition and analysis with Erwin Stein and Hans Keller. He went on to postgraduate studies at Glasgow University, and a lectureship at Southampton University Music Department. Like Tavener, his formative years as a young composer were in the 1960s, but in the rarefied atmosphere of 'academe', and away from the fashionable world of the capital.

His intellectual and analytical approach to composition was initially influenced by the music of Schoenberg, Berg and Messiaen, and later the ultramodernists Stockhausen and Babbitt, whom he came across as a Harkness Fellow at Princeton in 1969, but he was soon to develop a very personal style. The most striking feature of his mature music is the colourful and sensuous soundworld he creates, which belies the meticulous attention to detail and complex formal procedures behind it – 'spectralism', as he calls the process of linking the structure of sounds with the structure of the music. As well as his obvious musicality and sensitive ear, Harvey shows a profound spirituality in his compositions, all of which express a philosophical inquisitiveness and sincerity that makes an emotional as well as intellectual impact.

Slowly, through the 1970s, Harvey emerged as an important new voice in British music, with performances of his Cantatas and orchestral works such as *Persephone Dream* and *Inner Light* praised by the critics and admired by concert-goers and his fellow composers. Pierre Boulez, who had been based in London with the BBC Symphony Orchestra, was very impressed by Harvey, and invited him to work in the newly established IRCAM (Institut de Recherche et Co-ordination Acoustique/Musique) at the Pompidou Centre in Paris, an opportunity that allowed him to explore the possibilities of electro-acoustic music, expanding his musical palette. The association with IRCAM established him as a leading figure in electronic music, producing works such as *Bhakti* and *Mortuos Plango Vivos Voco*, in which he mixes and manipulates the recorded sounds of the great bell of Winchester Cathedral with the voice of his son (then a chorister at Winchester).

Harvey's catalogue of music has grown steadily since, and includes operas, works for orchestra, chorus and chamber ensembles, as well as electro-acoustic pieces. Commissions for new work still come from all over the world, and his music is regularly performed at the major music festivals and concert halls.

Meanwhile, he continued his academic career, becoming Professor of the progressive Music Department at Sussex University in 1980, a post he held for 18 years, enhancing the department's reputation for radical new music and providing an inspiration for the next generation of composers. He then took up a Professorship at Stanford University, California, and later became composer-in-residence with the BBC Scottish Symphony Orchestra, but maintains his connection with Sussex as Honorary Professor of Music.

It's tempting, when contrasting these two adopted Sussex composers, to make some sort of value judgement, but that would be unfair. Both Tavener and Harvey have achieved a place in the musical history books, and are well-respected for their work – and no-one can doubt the sincerity of the faith they express in their music. Yet the contrast between the two is striking: the extravert and fashionable Tavener, who still retains the hippy appearance he adopted in the 1960s, and has gained a popular following outside the narrow world of classical music; and the introvert and academic Harvey, owlish and conservatively dressed, respected by the cognoscenti but virtually unknown by the general public. And where Tavener is concerned with the ritual and ceremony of his faith, expressed in music he feels comes from divine inspiration, Harvey explores the philosophical basis of spirituality in his craftsman-like compositions. And that's the paradox – Tavener's music, despite his image as a cutting-edge composer, in fact has its roots in a deeply conservative and backward-looking tradition, while Harvey's less fashionable academic background has resulted in a music that is genuinely boundary-stretching and new.

Top Tunes
- ❯ TAVENER, *The Whale; Song for Athene; The Protecting Veil*
- ❯ HARVEY, *Inner Light; Bhakti; Mortuos Plango Vivos Voco*

SUSSEX ACADEME

RISE OF THE MODERNISTS

The new universities that sprang up in the 1960s seemed to be on a mission to shake up the cosy ivory tower image of the academic world. Campuses of modern buildings appeared in the countryside outside towns and cities all over Britain, and quickly established a reputation for rebellious new ideas. The University of Sussex transformed the sleepy little Downland village of Falmer, just north of Brighton, into a hotbed of radicalism, with an influx of free-thinking students and teachers.

The Music Department at Sussex, in its own way, was just as radical as the rest of the Humanities faculty. Founded in 1971, the department's first Professor was Donald Mitchell, a musicologist best known for his work on Mahler and Britten, but keen to attract the brightest stars of contemporary music on to his staff and encourage young composers to study at Sussex. Prominent on the teaching staff was David Osmond-Smith, whose enthusiasm for contemporary music and insightful research into composers such as Luciano Berio established the department as a centre for progressive music in the 1970s and continued until his death in 2007. Composition was an important part of the syllabus, with Australian composer Peter Sculthorpe a visiting professor, and when Donald Mitchell left in 1980, the appointment of Jonathan Harvey (*see pp.50-53*) as Professor put even more of an emphasis on new music. Internationally known composers were appointed to the staff, including Peter Wiegold, Michael Finnissy (*see p.56*), and Martin Butler (who was to take over as Professor after Harvey), teaching the next generation of composers – some of whom, like Julian Johnson, went on to teach at Sussex themselves.

Although primarily associated with contemporary classical music, the department isn't exclusively modernist; Reg Hall, a folk song enthusiast and champion of Scan Tester (*see p. 25*), was a visiting research fellow and gained his doctorate at Sussex. In addition, the University has conferred honorary degrees on Bob Copper and Paul McCartney.

The University has certainly stimulated interest in new music in Sussex generally and in Brighton in particular; there is a thriving music programme in its Centre of Continuing Education, and the formation of groups like New Music Brighton and the local branch of CoMA (Contemporary Music-making for Amateurs) has involved both town and gown. Music education has also improved across the county, not only with a greater emphasis on the subject in schools, but also through youth music centres and the East Sussex Academy of Music in Lewes.

Old Boys

A couple of independent schools in Sussex deserve mention here, both for their contribution to musical life in the county and for the musicians who were once pupils. Christ's Hospital, near Horsham, has a purpose-built auditorium that hosts a wide range of musical and theatrical productions, and boasts among its 'Old Blues' several musical celebrities: the composer and conductor Constant Lambert, conductors Colin Davis and Charles Hazlewood, songwriter Sydney Bertram Carter (best known for 'Lord of the Dance', set to the tune of Shaker hymn *Simple Gifts*), and the extraordinary folk-punk poet and musician John Baine, better known as Attila the Stockbroker.

Lancing College also has a reputation for music, much of it centred in the imposing chapel that dominates the local landscape; Benjamin Britten's cantata *Saint Nicolas* was written for the school's centenary celebrations in 1948. 'Old Lancings' include the tenor Peter Pears and librettist Tim Rice.

Brighton College is the Alma Mater of Gavin Henderson, one-time Principal of Trinity College of Music and Artistic Director of Dartington Summer School, who still lives in Brighton and has done much for the musical life in the city – he was Director of the Brighton Festival from 1984 to 1994 and heads several musical ventures in the city and is an Honorary Fellow of the Universities of Sussex and Brighton.

Top Places
- *Falmer and the University of Sussex*
- *Christ's Hospital, near Horsham*
- *Lancing College*

MICHAEL FINNISSY

*S*ome *may push and some may shuv, but Sussex men, they wunt be druv'*, as the local adage has it, and perhaps that's why Michael Finnissy (*born 1946*), an idiosyncratic composer of uncompromisingly modern music, has chosen to make his home here. Born in Tulse Hill, London, Finnissy came to the county in the late 1980s to teach composition at Sussex University, and has since settled in Steyning, on the Downs behind Brighton and Worthing, opting to remain a 'Sussex man' even when appointed Professor of Composition at Southampton University in 1999.

Finnissy is an accomplished pianist and an inspirational mentor, having taught at several colleges and universities and set up the department of music at the London School of Contemporary Dance, but it is as a prolific composer that he is best known. He started writing music at the age of four, taught by his great-aunt Rosie, and went on to study with Bernard Stevens and Humphrey Searle at the Royal College of Music and Roman Vlad in Italy, slowly (very slowly) finding an audience for his highly original music in the 1970s and 1980s. To make ends meet, he worked as a répétiteur, music-copyist and teacher, but even though he wasn't getting much public attention, he was certainly being noticed by other musicians – in 1990 he was elected President of the International Society for Contemporary Music.

Respect for his highly original compositions gradually spread from the rarefied academic world through the grapevine of new-music performers to the concert halls, and almost imperceptibly Finnissy emerged as one of the leading lights of contemporary music. Along with his friend and contemporary Brian Ferneyhough, he was initially pigeonholed as a founder of the 'New Complexity' school of composition, a term he dislikes but is still often saddled with because of the intricacy of his scores and the sometimes fearsome difficulty of performing them. Certainly his music is often complex, and 'difficult' too, in that it demands oncentration on the part of the audience, but the wide range of his musical interests and influences make it more 'approachable' than that of many other modernists.

His very personal and eclectic style, blending rigorous intellectualism and mathematical precision with improvisation-like spontaneity and a degree of indeterminacy, brings together elements of many musical cultures: there are references to folk music, jazz and popular music, and the stylistic mannerisms of 'classical' music from its beginnings to the 20th-century avant garde. As well as his original compositions, he has made arrangements of the work of composers as diverse as Obrecht, Verdi and Gershwin, which attest to his love and understanding of their music and make a very accessible introduction to his work.

Morgan Hayes

A one-time pupil of Finnissy's, Morgan Hayes (*born 1973*) has already established an enviable reputation, despite composing in an unfashionably modernist style. Hayes was born and brought up in Hastings and showed an interest in composition and new music at an early age. He learnt the piano with local composer David Branson and as a teenager was encouraged to pursue his career as a composer by the judges at the Hastings Music Festival, who were impressed by his work. After studies in Lewes, and privately with Finnissy, he went to the Guildhall School of Music & Drama where he was taught by Simon Bainbridge and Robert Saxton, and by the mid-1990s had developed a distinctly personal musical language. Performances and recordings of his work became more high-profile, culminating in *Strip*, a breakthrough commission for the 2006 Proms, which was his first work for full orchestra, and enthusiastically praised by the critics.

Top Place
> *Steyning, Michael Finnissy's home*

Top Tunes
> FINNISSY, *The History of Photography in Sound; Gershwin arrangements for piano; Seven Sacred Motets; Folklore and Folklore II*
> HAYES, *Original Version; Strip*

SUSSEX VIRTUOSI

ORCHESTRAL MANOEUVRES

Inevitably, large cities tend to be the centres of musical life and performers looking to make their name are drawn from the provinces to the concert halls, opera houses, orchestras and music colleges based in them. Other than Brighton, Sussex has only comparatively small towns and is a predominantly rural county, not within easy commuting distance from the capital – at least, not for musicians whose work involves late-night and weekend travelling. So it's no surprise to find that only very few have chosen to live this far from their work and many Sussex-born musicians have moved away.

That's not say that there aren't many professional musicians working in the county – far from it – but it tends be the home of leading performers only at the beginning, or end, of their careers; there are limited opportunities for anybody wanting to achieve anything more than local fame in Sussex, especially with the demise of many municipal orchestras after World War II. Before then, seaside resorts often had very fine resident orchestras with well known conductors, such as the Brighton Philharmonic Orchestra under Herbert Menges from 1925 to as recently as 1972, and the Hastings Municipal Orchestra led by Julius Harrison in the 1930s.

Among the conductors who have succeeded elsewhere, a good handful started out in the county, including Colin Davis (*born 1927*) and Charles Hazlewood, both Christ's Hospital 'Old Blues', and Sussex-born Mark Wigglesworth (*born 1964*). One who ended up in Sussex is the Naples-born Michael Costa (*1808-84*), conductor at Covent Garden and the Philharmonic Society, who died in Hove.

The most celebrated singer from Sussex is undoubtedly Clara Butt (*see pp.60-61*), closely followed by the tenor Peter Pears (*1910-86*), who began his singing career while at school in Lancing College, and countertenor Alfred Deller (*1912-79*), who lived in St Leonards-on-Sea in the 1930s, where his son Mark (also a countertenor) was born in 1938. Coincidentally St Leonards is also the birthplace of tenor Neil Jenkins (*born 1945*).

Instrumentalists with Sussex links include the pianist Peter Katin (*born 1930*), renowned especially for his interpretations of Chopin who, after many years of association with the area, has retired to Bexhill – although retirement has not stopped him continuing an active programme of recitals and recordings. Similarly, Ronald Smith (*1922-2004*), who had a second home in Hastings Old Town for many years, didn't let his retirement get in the way of his career as a pianist and teacher. For home-grown talent, there is also pianist and broadcaster David Owen Norris, who comes from Elgar's Sussex retreat, Fittleworth.

To ensure the contribution of the accompanist isn't overlooked (as it so often is), we have David Willison, for many years a resident of Rye and Artistic Director of the Rye Festival, known for his recordings with singers Benjamin Luxon and Anthony Rolfe Johnson.

Instrument makers

Behind the scenes, a whole army of talented craftsmen and technicians makes its contribution to musical life in Sussex. As well as the many repairers, restorers and tuners maintaining local performers' instruments, there are very skilled makers who supply instruments well beyond the confines of the county. Violin makers include Restalls in Midhurst, Peter Voigt (a family firm that has been in Lindfield since the 17th century), and Godfrey Sheppard, who specialises in double basses. For many years, bowmaker Brian Tunnicliffe operated from his home in Sedlescombe; Bruce I Brook makes lutes, baroque guitars and the like in Windmill Hill, Herstmonceux, and John Paul has a harpsichord workshop in Waldron, Heathfield. There's even an organ maker, Wood Brown, in Burgess Hill, and the Stanhope Collection in Winchelsea has both original and reproduction early keyboard instruments available for performances. For budding instrument makers, West Dean College, between Chichester and Midhurst, runs courses in early instrument making.

CLASSICAL BEAUTIES

WOMEN MUSICIANS

I t will not have escaped the reader's notice that little mention has been made so far of female classical musicians in Sussex. Nevertheless, of those who have achieved fame in this predominantly male domain, several outstanding figures have Sussex connections.

First, and probably foremost, of these women musicians is Clara Butt (*1872-1936*), who was born in Southwick. Her father, Henry Butt, was a captain in the merchant Navy and a keen amateur singer, and music-making was an important part of family life for the Butts. By the time they moved to Bristol in 1880, it was already apparent that Clara possessed an extraordinary (and powerful) voice, which with a little training enabled her to get a scholarship to the Royal College of Music in 1890. Although originally a soprano, Clara was also capable of singing alto, and it was the remarkably sonorous quality of the lower end of her register that got her noticed (although, being over six feet tall, and strikingly good-looking, she was difficult to ignore). In a very short time, she became a star of concert halls and opera houses, much in demand as a soloist in oratorios, and a favourite of the Royal Family. Elgar, who had already written a song cycle for her, added the now familiar words of 'Land of Hope and Glory' by A.C. Benson to his D major '*Pomp and Circumstance*' march, providing her with a song that became one of the first best-selling gramophone records. She was made a Dame of the British Empire in 1920 and continued performing until her death.

Running parallel to the career of Dame Clara, the rise to fame (and notoriety) of Violet Gordon Woodhouse (*1871-1948*) was remarkable not only for her success in a male-dominated profession, but also for pioneering the use of harpsichords and clavichords in performance of early music. Oh, and also because she lived in a happy *ménage à cinq* with four 'husbands', and inherited a fortune with her (legal) husband,

Gordon Woodhouse, when his sisters were murdered by their butler. She was born in London but in 1876 moved to Folkington, where she lived until the 1920s. Violet was an accomplished pianist by the age of seven, and in the late 1890s became interested in early English music, which at that time was played on the piano. After lessons with Arnold Dolmetsch, the early music scholar, she decided that this music deserved more authentic performance, and took up the harpsichord and clavichord, neglected since the advent of the piano in the 18th century. She was the first modern performer to record the instruments, and became famous for her harpsichord recitals. Inheritance of the Woodhouse wealth in the late 1920s enabled her to move to a splendid manor house in Gloucestershire and return to private music making. After her death in London, she was buried in Folkington churchyard.

Women composers

Ruth Gipps (*1921-99*) was born at the Bexhill School of Music, where her mother was Principal, and returned to Sussex in retirement, dying in Eastbourne. She studied at the Royal College of Music (RCM), played in the City of Birmingham Orchestra, taught composition at Trinity College and the RCM, and was famous for driving her open-topped vintage sports cars in all weathers. She was a well-respected musical educator, but despite being a prolific composer in all genres, often struggled to get her music performed. Louise Denny (*born 1947*), now based in St Leonards-on-Sea, has had more luck in getting her music performed, although she got off to a shaky start by writing a concert march for the SAS before realising the regiment didn't have a band. Nevertheless, she has since become, unusually for a woman, well known for her military marches, and has also written several works for orchestra, including *Violette*, a tribute to the French resistance agent Violette Szabo.

Top Places
❯ *Southwick, birthplace of Clara Butt*
❯ *Folkington churchyard, burial place of Violet Gordon Woodhouse*

Top Tunes
❯ CLARA BUTT, *'Land of Hope and Glory'*
❯ VIOLET GORDON WOODHOUSE, *'Great Virtuosi of the Harpsichord'* Volume III CD
❯ RUTH GIPPS, *Symphony No. 2*
❯ LOUISE DENNY, *Violette*

WINIFRED WAGNER

SPRINGTIME FOR HITLER

The contribution Hastings has made to the Bayreuth Festival is not often acknowleged – the uncomfortable truth is that Winifred Wagner (*1897-1980*), the matriarchal figure at the helm of the Bayreuth Festival through the Nazi years, was a Sussex girl.

She started life as Winifred Williams, daughter of Hastings writer John Williams, but was orphaned before the age of two and taken into care. Her health was fragile, and she was moved from orphanage to orphanage over the next few years, until she was tracked down by Henrietta Karop, a member of the German side of her mother's family, and adopted by her and her husband Karl Klindworth. Winifred was taken from the orphanage in East Grinstead to Germany, where Klindworth was moderately well known as a violinist and conductor, and a friend of Richard Wagner. Now known as Winifred Klindworth, she grew up surrounded by music, but also rabid anti-semitism.

Meanwhile, the Wagner family was going through something of a crisis. After Richard died in 1883, the festival of his operas he had set up in Bayreuth was run by his son Siegfried, but this proved problematic, as Siegfried was homosexual – which didn't square up to the macho image of Bayreuth, and was totally beyond the pale in turn-of-the-century Germany. Siegfried's proclivities were hushed up and the family decided that he should marry to avoid any rumours and to provide an heir. With this in mind, he was introduced to Winifred at the Festival in 1914, and despite an age difference of 28 years, they were married the following year.

Winifred kept her side of the bargain, producing four children (Wieland, Friedelinde, Wolfgang and Verena) in the next five years, but Siegfried continued (more or less discreetly) with his homosexual affairs. The fruitful marriage did at least provide an efficient smokescreen to prevent any public scandal, and Siegfried was sufficiently socially acceptable to run the Festival until his death in 1930.

By this time Winifred was in a powerful position, not only as the head of the Wagner family (with the key to a cupboardful of skeletons), but also because she had friends in high places – one of her most ardent admirers was the up-and-coming Adolf Hitler. There was, then, no opposition to her taking over the running of Bayreuth, and the Festival flourished in the 1930s under her leadership, helped, no doubt, by government support: when Hitler became Chancellor, Bayreuth benefited from generous grants and exemption from taxes.

The fervent nationalism of Richard Wagner's operas suited Nazi-ruled Germany, and Winifred's English roots were overlooked. She remained head of the Festival through World War II, although it was effectively run by the Nazi party as a propaganda tool, but after Hitler's defeat was banned from Bayreuth by a war court. Controversially, the Festival was allowed to continue under the direction of her two sons.

Unrepentant about her close relationship with Hitler, but denying any involvement with the Nazi party or the Holocaust, Winifred Wagner died in Überlingen, on Lake Constance, aged 82, and is buried at Bayreuth – a long way from Hastings.

Hitler

Adolf Hitler was a great fan of Richard Wagner's music and knew the family well. From the 1920s, he was a frequent guest at Haus Wahnfried, the Wagner home in Bayreuth, and was very taken with Winifred (he apparently even proposed to her on several occasions after Siegfried died). She became a close friend and staunch supporter of his nationalist politics, although she later denied any involvement with the Nazi party and professed to being appalled by his persecution of the Jews. When Hitler was imprisoned, she sent him food parcels and, so the story goes, writing paper on which he wrote *Mein Kampf*, and later acted as his interpreter in the diplomatic negotiations with Britain leading up to World War II.

Top Read
❯ Brigitte Hamann, *Winifred Wagner: A Life at the Heart of Hitler's Bayreuth*, (Harcourt, 2005)

SUSSEX ENSEMBLES

THE PERFORMING ARTS

G one are the days, sadly, when there was a professional orchestra and a concert season in every moderately-sized town, especially the seaside resorts hoping to attract what are now known as 'cultural tourists'. It's an expensive business keeping even chamber groups in one place and few towns can afford the luxury of a permanent resident orchestra, so professional ensembles these days are more likely to attach themselves to concert halls or teaching institutions in major cities or resign themselves to a life of touring. A few have survived in Sussex, however, but now often with professional players who also have full-time commitments elsewhere, only coming together on an *ad hoc* basis, or formed from a mixture of professionals and amateurs. There are also a healthy number of amateur ensembles performing to very professional standards.

Brighton, of course, is best able to provide the necessary audiences, and is home to several orchestras. Foremost among the professional ensembles are: The Hanover Band, resident in the Old Market in Hove, which is recognised as one of the leading period-instrument orchestras in the world, performing a mainly Baroque and Classical repertoire; the Brighton Philharmonic Orchestra, which started out in 1925 as the Brighton Symphonic String Players and has been playing regularly at the Dome and elsewhere ever since; and also based in Brighton is the Sussex Symphony Orchestra, formed in 1993 and giving concerts across the region. Worthing still boasts a concert series from its own Worthing Symphony Orchestra.

The line between professional and amateur becomes a little blurred with many of the other ensembles performing in Sussex: the Musicians of All Saints in Lewes, Chichester Symphony Orchestra and Brighton Chamber Orchestra all have a core of professionals and very proficient amateurs, and there are amateur ensembles throughout the county with some professional players, or retired musicians wanting to keep their hand in.

Choirs and choruses also abound in Sussex, as do performances of choral music with and without orchestral accompaniment. There are literally dozens of choral societies, philharmonic choirs, choruses and consorts, based in almost every town across the county.

Although Glyndebourne quite rightly dominates the opera scene locally, a couple of other companies have managed to make their mark too. New Sussex Opera has staged impressive and ambitious productions since its formation in 1978, touring through Sussex and sometimes beyond, and Opera South East puts on two operas (sung in English) a year at its base in Hastings and in other venues in the south east.

Music Festivals in Sussex

The Sussex Festival season is dominated by the two big ones, Glyndebourne (see pp.82-85) and the Brighton Festival, which have an international reputation and feature world class performers, but there's a lot more going on too.

Many are festivals of all the arts, with exhibitions, theatre, poetry readings and all kinds of events as well as concerts. 'Classical' music plays a greater or lesser part from place to place, alongside folk, jazz, rock, and world music. The Brighton Festival, held annually in May, is by far the biggest of this kind, but there are similar events in Eastbourne and Chichester, and smaller ones in Battle, Rye, East Grinstead, Horsham, Petworth and Adur – and even in villages such as Etchingham.

Purely musical festivals are rarer: Glyndebourne, devoted exclusively to opera, is a rather special case, as are the Brighton Early Music Festival, Soundwaves Festival of new music (also in Brighton) and the Florestan Festival of chamber music in Peasmarsh, just outside Rye, but all are significant dates in the calendar for anybody interested in those particular genres. More participatory, but still offering the chance of some high-class performances, are the competitive music festivals: Springboard (formerly the Brighton & Hove Competitive Musical Festival), Mid-Sussex Competitive Music Festival, and the Hastings Musical Festival. These provide a good opportunity not just for the competitors, but for audiences to catch local performers at the beginning of their careers.

SUSSEX
POP

As you'd expect in a county whose income is largely reliant on the tourism and entertainment of its coastal resorts, there's a lot of 'popular music' in Sussex. Contrary to the conservative image many outsiders have of the county, however, this music for the masses is not just tolerated but, well… popular. Audiences for variety shows, jazz and rock concerts and pub bands contain as many residents as visitors, and as often as not the performers are locals. What's more Sussex is also home to a good deal of cutting-edge stuff, particularly in the jazz and progressive rock fields.

From the early days of music hall, the south coast, and in particular Brighton, has taken a leading role. Variety acts strove to get into the Sussex resorts as much as the London stages and Victorian stars were regular visitors here. Before long, Sussex was producing its own music-hall stars, the greatest of all being Max Miller.

With the advent of cinema, then radio and TV, a new breed of stars came along, and a new kind of music. Big bands and jazz were the order of the day. Sussex rose to the challenge of providing musicians as well as audiences for the new style. Composers such as Eric Coates and Charles Williams turned their hands to writing music for the movies and radio, and later TV gave Ron Grainer and Howard Blake their big breaks.

And when popular music became pop, there was no shortage of Sussex talent. From Alma Cogan in the 1950s to Keane in the new century, local pop and rock musicians made it to the big time. Brighton's lively pop, rock and disco scene brought in a lot of famous names, and the lower-profile but no less active jazz, folk and blues scene (and a notoriously bohemian arts community) in Hastings attracted yet more.

VARIETY PERFORMERS

MUSIC HALL MECCA

Music Halls, with their cheeky humour and popular song-and-dance routines, were ideally suited to the holiday atmosphere of seaside towns and thrived in the resorts along the Sussex coast before the advent of cinema, radio and TV. And nowhere more so than Brighton, whose variety theatres were a Mecca for audiences and performers in Victorian and Edwardian times.

The top-of-the bill performers were usually singers, offering renditions of the latest popular ballads and singalong numbers, but the real crowd-pullers were comedians, whose routines were often satirically topical and quite risqué, even by today's standards. Their acts almost always included a song or two, or a song-and-dance routine – often written by the performer. Among the stars treading the boards in Sussex was the male impersonator Vesta Tilley (*1864-1952*), singer of comic songs such as 'Girls Are the Ruin of Men' and 'Angels Without Wings', who was fond enough of Brighton to spend her honeymoon there and, in her eighties, to buy a holiday home in Hove. Billy Williams (*1878-1915*) came to Britain from Australia in 1899 and in a tragically short career as a comic singer became one of the first best-selling recording artists, as well as topping the bill in the music halls. He died in Hove after an unsuccessful operation, and is buried in Shoreham – coincidentally the same resting place as Ernie Mayne (*1874-1937*), whose song 'What D'ye Think of That' became the basis for Lonnie Donnegan's 1950s hit 'My Old Man's a Dustman'.

Brought up with acts like theirs regularly on his doorstep, it's not surprising that a Brighton lad, Max Miller (*1894-1963*), should become the undisputed king of music-hall entertainers. Although remembered for his 'Cheeky Chappie' comedy routines, he started out as a song-and-dance man, and incorporated several self-penned songs into his act.

Chesney Allen (*1893-1982*) was also born in Brighton and shared Miller's background in the music halls. He made his name as a member of the Crazy Gang (with Bud Flanagan, Jimmy Nervo, Teddy Knox, Charlie Naughton, Jimmy Gold and 'Monsewer' Eddie Gray) in the 1930s, appearing with them in several successful wartime films. Flanagan and Allen also performed separately from the team, invariably finishing with a song, with Allen's gruff, almost spoken delivery providing the harmony to Flanagan's crooning: comic songs such as 'We're Going to Hang Out the Washing On the Siegfried Line', and the sentimental 'Miss You' and 'Underneath the Arches' were wartime hits for the duo. Allen died in Midhurst in 1982 and is commemorated by a plaque in Chichester Cathedral, where he is buried.

Flanagan and Allen weren't the only ones to find success with the wartime thirst for sentimental songs. Vera Lynn (*born 1917*) became known as 'The Forces' Sweetheart' for her renditions of 'We'll Meet Again' and 'The White Cliffs of Dover', and remained popular well after the end of the war, receiving a DBE in 1975.

The Boys in the Band

Radio broadcasts of variety shows contributed to the demise of the music hall, with studio bands and singers making bandleaders into international stars. Ray Noble (*1903-78*) was born in Brighton, but made his name in the U.S. with his own band and penning 'Love is the Sweetest Thing' and 'The Very Thought of You'. Other band-leaders featured on British radio, included Battle-born Frank Chacksfield (*1914-95*), and Geoff Love (*1917-91*), who for many years lived in Hastings, and often performed with his orchestra under the name 'Manuel and his Music of the Mountains'.

Top Places
- The Max Miller statue in New Road, Brighton, outside the Theatre Royal
- Ditchling, home of Vera Lynn
- Chesney Allen plaque in Chichester Cathedral

Top Tunes
- ERNIE MAYNE, 'What D'ye Think of That'
- BILLY WILLIAMS, 'When Father Papered the Parlour'
- MAX MILLER, 'Mary From the Dairy'
- CHESNEY ALLEN (with Bud Flanagan) 'Underneath the Arches'

JAZZ

THE SUSSEX JAZZ SCENE

The history of jazz is a relatively short one, spanning less than a century so far, and even shorter in Britain, where it was not until the 1940s that it really made any impact. American servicemen brought the new music here during World War II, in the rather diluted form of swing bands such as Glenn Miller's, and it rapidly replaced the very staid dance bands we had been used to. It also opened the floodgates to an invasion of American music, starting a craze for crooners and big bands, but also creating a market hungry for some real jazz. The 'trad revival' of the 1950s resulted from the discovery of New Orleans-style 'Dixieland' jazz, but even then, some young British fans had already cottoned on to postwar developments in the US – bebop had replaced swing, and this was the era of 'modern' jazz.

As ever, the latest trends took a while to filter down to Sussex from London, but jazz soon caught on in the 1950s, especially in towns like Brighton and Hastings. Trad bands sprang up all over the county, and former dance band players jumped on to the much more exciting bandwagon. One, who had cut his teeth in the Billy Cotton band, was trumpeter and vocalist Nat Gonella (*1908-98*), a stalwart of the Brighton jazz scene and resident of Saltdean. He was a significant influence on the younger generation of jazz players that were appearing at the time, especially Humphrey Lyttleton, whose band included on clarinet a young cartoonist, Wally Fawkes (*born 1924*), who has lived in Hastings for many years. Fawkes, under the pseudonym Trog, created the cartoon character Flook for the *Daily Mail* in 1949, with story lines by Lyttleton, and later fellow jazzer George Melly, who frequently visited Hastings.

Although trad remains popular, with people of a certain age at least, the 1960s saw it being replaced by pop and rock as the music of choice of young people, and aficionados' tastes had matured to a diet of modern jazz, but this was something of a minority pursuit. Jazz clubs and pubs provided a platform for emerging local players and have survived into the 21st century, perhaps even more healthily than before. In Brighton, trumpeter Ian Hamer kept the jazz flag flying, forming the Sussex Jazz Orchestra in 1987; and pianist Terry Seabrook and saxophonist Geoff Simkins are both very active in the jazz scene in their home town of Brighton.

Legendary figures moved to Sussex in the 1970s and 1980s, revitalising the local jazz community. Trevor Watts, saxophonist with the Spontaneous Music Ensemble and London Jazz Composers' Orchestra, moved to an already lively jazz scene in Hastings, and formed his Moiré Music from largely local talent, including drummer Liam Genockey, percussionist Nana Tsiboe, violinist Peter Knight, pianist Liane Carroll and Colin Gibson on bass; later line-ups included saxophonist Marcus Cummins, bassist Roger Carey and percussionist Jamie Harris. One of the 'grand old men' of British jazz, tenor-player Bobby Wellins, settled in Felpham and often appeared at Sussex jazz clubs. Pianist John Donaldson and bassist Herbie Flowers have also made Sussex their home.

Liane Carroll & Claire Martin

Hastings born and bred, and still playing regularly in her home town, Liane Carroll has become one of the town's favourite exports. Headlining at Ronnie Scott's Jazz Club since 1993, she found a wider audience with her album *Billy No Mates* in 2003, which earned her two BBC Jazz Awards, Best Vocalist and Best of Jazz, in 2005 and she later won Best Female Jazz Vocalist in the first Ronnie Scott's Jazz Awards. As well as her solo piano and vocal act, she fronts a trio, with husband Roger Carey on bass and drummer Mark Fletcher.

Another award-winning vocalist, Claire Martin, is based in Brighton. Best Vocalist at the British Jazz Awards an astonishing five times, Claire tours internationally and also co-presents *Jazz Line Up* on BBC Radio 3.

Top Tunes
- NAT GONELLA, *'Georgia on my Mind'*
- TREVOR WATTS, *'With One Voice'*
- BOBBY WELLINS *(with Stan Tracey), Jazz Suite inspired by Dylan Thomas's Under Milk Wood*

LIGHTS, CAMERA, ACTION

MUSIC FOR RADIO, TV & CINEMA

Some pieces of music are so well known through their appearance in films or as themes for TV and radio that they have a wider (and more enduring) audience than even the best-selling pop hits – the tunes that almost everyone recognises, but can seldom put a name to, let alone a composer. The creators of these popular gems have a very special talent which often goes unnoticed. And, as you might expect, several of them have Sussex connections.

A good example is the theme tune for Radio 4's *Desert Island Discs*: instantly recognisable, but few people know its title *By the Sleepy Lagoon*, or that it was written by Eric Coates (*1886-1957*), who also composed the theme for *Music While You Work* (entitled *Calling all Workers*) and the title march to the film *The Dam Busters*. Coates had a house in Selsey in the 1920s and 1930s, and it was the view from the east beach across the bay to Bognor that inspired *By the Sleepy Lagoon* in 1930 – there's a commemorative blue plaque on the seafront marking the spot. Later he and his family moved to Sidlesham, south of Chichester, where he composed much of his music for radio, TV and the cinema. For more than a decade a Coates march could be heard daily as the start-up theme for BBC TV, prompting commercial stations to commission Coates for their opening music, imprinting the tunes in the memories of a whole generation.

Less well known today, except by the generation brought up with the adventures of *Dick Barton, Special Agent* on the BBC Light Programme, is the music of Charles Williams (*1893-1978*) who composed the frantic theme *Devil's Gallop* – still used in pastiche radio thrillers. Williams was born in Findon Valley, Worthing, and studied at the Royal Academy of Music, becoming a respected conductor of light music as well as composing music for many films of the 1930s and 1940s. His contribution was often uncredited, but he became practically a household name when his piano concerto-like soundtrack to *While I Live* became a hit in its own right in 1947 as *The Dream of Olwen*.

More recently, an Australian-born composer came near to achieving immortality with one of his many television theme tunes. Ron Grainer (*1922-81*), composer of the *Doctor Who* theme, came to England in 1952, working first as a pianist and musical adviser for TV companies. His big break came when he was asked to compose the music for the *Maigret* series in 1960, which led to further BBC commissions, including *Old Ned* (the theme tune to *Steptoe and Son*) and the *Doctor Who* theme, realised by Delia Derbyshire in the BBC Radiophonic Workshop; the commercial stations also offered him work, and he provided them with title music for the series *Man in a Suitcase*, *The Prisoner* and *Tales of the Unexpected*. He settled in Brighton in the 1970s, but died in Cuckfield in 1981, aged only 58.

Howard Blake (*born 1938*) is similarly famous for one song in particular, but he is in fact a prolific composer of film and concert music. His scores for films such as *Flash Gordon* got him noticed by the industry, but it was the music for the animated feature of Raymond Briggs's *The Snowman*, and especially the song 'Walking in the Air', that earned him public attention as well as a BAFTA award and an Oscar nomination in 1982. Born in London, Blake was brought up in Brighton, winning a scholarship through the Hastings Musical Festival to the Royal Academy of Music. He returned to Sussex in 1971, living in Highbridge Mill, Cuckfield for ten years, and he still lives and works in the county.

Top Places
- Selsey, blue plaque on east beach commemorating the view that inspired Eric Coates
- Findon Valley, birthplace of Charles Williams
- Cuckfield, where Ron Grainer died, and Howard Blake lived in Highbridge Mill

Top Tunes
- ERIC COATES, *By the Sleepy Lagoon; The Dam Busters March*
- CHARLES WILLIAMS, *The Dream of Olwen*
- RON GRAINER, *Doctor Who; Old Ned*
- HOWARD BLAKE, *Flash Gordon; The Snowman*

ROCK & POP

THE SUSSEX HIT PARADE

Popular music is by its nature fashion-led, and essentially ephemeral. Not only the music, but the musicians too; after a brief spell in the limelight, the majority disappear into obscurity – but a select few have achieved enduring fame. Of these, a surprising number either come from Sussex or have made their homes here.

Pop music as such didn't appear until the 1950s, and when the 'hit parade' charts of record sales were first published, they were often dominated not by teenage rock'n'roll, but more family-friendly crooners. Donald Peers (*1908-73*), who died in a Brighton nursing home, was in his forties and already established as a big band singer when he became just such an unlikely pop idol in the early 1950s. Perhaps more surprisingly, in 1959 a pub-style pianist, Russ Conway (*1925-2000*), pushed Elvis off the number one spot and remained in the charts into the Swinging Sixties with hit singles such as 'Side Saddle' and 'Roulette'. He moved to Eastbourne in the 1990s, and continued to perform despite recurrent stomach cancer until his death, aged 75, in 2000.

But there was no holding back the pop revolution, spearheaded by singers such as Alma Cogan (*1932-66*), the girl from Worthing who had a string of hits from 1954 to her untimely death; the perennial favourite Cliff Richard, for a short time a Sussex resident, whose backing band The Shadows had Bognor-born Bruce Welch on guitar; and Adam Faith (*1940-2003*), singer-turned-actor-turned-financial journalist (and discoverer and manager of another Sussex star, Leo Sayer, from Shoreham), who lived in Hartfield and Henfield and had a long association with Brighton.

Sixties superstars often chose Sussex as a place they could get away to. Paul McCartney (*born 1941*), moved with his family to a farm in Peasmarsh, outside Rye, in the 1970s (he also has an honorary degree from the University of Sussex), and soon became an accepted part of the local community – as has Arthur Brown in his adopted home of Lewes, despite the aggressively manic image as frontman of the Crazy World of Arthur Brown.

The progressive rock that followed on from the psychedelic late 1960s brought its share of stars too, among them Keith Emerson (*born 1944*), keyboard player with The Nice and Emerson Lake and Palmer, who grew up in Worthing; and Judge Smith (*born 1948*), who started his career as drummer in prog-rock band Van der Graaf Generator, and went on to carve a successful career as a composer of musicals and rock operas, including the extraordinary 'songstory' *Curly's Airships* (the story of the R101 airship disaster in 1930), from his home in Polegate.

Brighton has always been a popular base for celebrities, and these days boasts a host of pop- and rock-star residents, and the founding of the Brighton Institute of Modern Music (BIMM) in 2003 has started some local bands on the road to possible stardom. Perhaps the most unusual group to come out of the city (and the most typically Brighton) is the dance/percussion troupe Stomp, founded by Luke Cresswell and Steve McNicholas in 1991. Stomp's members play their own accompanying music as they dance, by stamping, kicking or hitting all manner of everyday objects from dustbins and their lids to bicycles and lampposts, with sticks, brooms – anything that will make a satisfactory noise.

The Frith Brothers

Fred Frith (*born 1949*) is one musician who defies categorisation, having started out in avant-garde rock band Henry Cow and made his name as a multi-instrumentalist and composer in the worlds of rock, free improvisation and modern 'classical' music. Born in Heathfield, he now lives in the U.S., and is Professor of Composition at Mills College in Oakland, California, but still performs worldwide. His brother Simon was for some years a rock critic, later a sociologist with a special interest in popular culture, the author of *The Sociology of Rock* in 1978, and became Tovey Professor of Music at Edinburgh University in 2006.

Top Places
- Peasmarsh, *Paul McCartney's home village*
- Heathfield, *birthplace of the Frith brothers*

BRIAN JONES

SINK LIKE A STONE

In a very short time after their formation in 1962, the Rolling Stones had become second only to the Beatles in popularity, and members of the band were wealthy young men. Like many rock stars, they each used some of their fortune to acquire a country home in the mid-1960s. Mick Jagger bought a house in Berkshire that had once belonged to Oliver Cromwell, Bill Wyman a house in Suffolk, and the others found places in Sussex: Charlie Watts bought a house near Lewes from Lord Shawcross, Keith Richards purchased property in West Wittering, and Brian Jones acquired a farm near Hartfield in November 1968.

Cotchford Farm was the first property that Brian Jones (*1942-69*) had ever owned and he regarded it as a sanctuary he could retreat to, and a welcome change from the rented flats, hotel rooms and rehab clinics he had inhabited previously. The house was a rambling Sussex country farmhouse, set in beautiful countryside in Ashdown Forest, and had been the home of A.A. Milne, author of the Winnie the Pooh stories; for Jones, it must have represented more than just a status symbol – it was somewhere he could get away to in order to sort out the mess that his life had become. Little had been going well for him. He had become increasingly dependent on alcohol and drugs and had been arrested twice for possession of cannabis, cocaine and LSD. Partly because of his drug abuse, but also through musical differences, he was estranged from the Stones – it didn't help that his girlfriend, Anita Pallenburg, had run off with Keith Richards – and he was at a crossroads in his musical career.

The Stones were scheduled to tour the US in late 1969, but Jones's police record prevented him getting a work permit and the band told him in June that they would carry on without him, taking on guitarist Mick Taylor in his place.

There are conflicting stories as to what happened next. Some say that he had plans to join another band with Alexis Korner, others that he intended to form a new band. Friends said that he was happy and well, but there were reports that he was turning to drugs and alcohol even more. Whatever his state of mind was, he and his girlfriend Anna Wohlin spent the next month at Cotchford, with a local builder, Frank Thorogood, staying at the house to oversee renovations.

On 3rd July, at about midnight, Jones, aged 27, was found at the bottom of his swimming pool. By the time doctors arrived he was dead. At an inquest, the coroner's verdict was death by misadventure, but there was inevitably controversy surrounding the incident: was it a tragic accident, the result of years of substance abuse, or could it have been suicide? Or, as Wohlin claimed later, murder? It was true that Jones had fallen out with the builders working on the house and the Stones' driver claimed that Thorogood had made a deathbed confession to Jones's murder in the late 1990s but the matter was never resolved.

Cotchford Farmhouse no longer exists: subsequent owners found it too expensive to maintain, and replaced it with a new building.

Hammerwood House

The Rolling Stones were not the only rock stars to buy high-class property in Sussex. In 1973 Led Zeppelin collectively acquired a magnificent country home, Hammerwood House near East Grinstead, to use as communal accommodation for the group and their families. It was built in 1792 by Benjamin Latrobe, his first major work and one of the earliest examples of the Greek Revival style in England, but its architectural merit was underrated at the time and the band bought it for (possibly literally) a song. A tour of North America took the musicians' mind off the project, and then they completely forgot that they owned the property, which fell into disrepair over the next couple of decades. It was sold and restored in 1982 and today continues its musical history as the home of the Harrison Trust, dedicated to the memory of the Harrison sisters, a family of musicians from Limpsfield, Surrey.

Top Tunes
◎ THE ROLLING STONES, 'Little Red Rooster' (featuring Jones on slide guitar); 'Ruby Tuesday' (Jones on recorder); 'Lady Jane' (Jones on dulcimer)

A GOOD NIGHT OUT

MUSICAL VENUES

Sadly, the music halls have almost completely disappeared from Sussex, although some of the buildings remain either as theatres or cinemas, or, like the Hippodrome in Hastings, ending their days ignominiously as amusement arcades. But variety shows are still popular, especially in the resort towns, and holiday seasons in the theatres and concert halls along the coast still have some of the atmosphere of the music hall and end-of-the-pier show.

It's also in the theatres and concert halls that you're most likely to find easy-listening orchestras and big bands, now that the dance palaces are no longer financially viable – the big auditoriums all over Sussex have had to cater for all tastes in order to stay open themselves, putting on everything from opera and classical music to tribute bands and rock groups, as well as drama and stand-up comedy. But, it has to be said, the quality of the acts in many of these is at best variable, as poor audiences in the smaller towns can't attract the big names. The exception, of course, is Brighton, which is big enough (and accessible enough from elsewhere in the county) to sustain several venues, notably the Dome and Corn Exchange, which bring in world-class musicians.

When it comes to jazz, though, Sussex fares better than most of the rest of the country outside London. As well as the major concerts in Brighton, there are many well known pubs and clubs across the county regularly hosting the best British players in more informal surroundings – which are probably better suited to the genre anyway, even though they are somewhat hampered by English licensing laws. There's usually a strong local feel to these venues, with resident (or at least regular) local bands, often of a very high standard, but also frequent gigs by high-profile guest performers. While some pubs have long established jazz connections, like the Hare and Hounds in Worthing, others come and go, so it's a good idea to check with local papers and gig guides before embarking on a night out in unknown territory, or you could end up with a karaoke session or worse. Brighton has always had a good number of venues for jazz of all sorts, but the presence in Hastings of some outstanding players has prompted some of the best jazz in the county, with regular jazz spots in several pubs, Pissarro's in the town centre being the best known, and a couple of jazz clubs showcasing top performers.

Naturally, none of these venues could survive on jazz alone and the majority also devote other nights to different live music. Although many of the night-clubs rely on recorded music and DJs, there are some that feature live bands, and a healthy proportion of Sussex pubs, in the villages as well as the towns, have live rock and blues bands, especially at the weekends. It would be impossible to list them all, and quite probably pointless too, as venues change almost as frequently as fashions in music, but they can soon be tracked down with the help of the numerous *What's On* guides to different areas in Sussex.

If you're looking for big-name bands though, you're going to be disappointed unless you go to the Dome in Brighton or the Hawth in Crawley, or if there happens to be a one-off outdoor concert somewhere – Sussex is not as high on the list of tour venues for major stars as it was in the 1960s, when mods, rockers, hippies and all sorts flocked down at every available opportunity.

Top Places

- *Komedia, Gardner Street, Brighton*
- *Joogleberry Playhouse, Manchester Street, Brighton*
- *Concorde 2, Madeira Drive, Kemptown, Brighton*
- *The Gloucester, Gloucester Place, Brighton*
- *The Lift, Queens Road, Brighton*
- *Pissarro's, South Terrace, Hastings*
- *Hare & Hounds, Portland Road, Worthing*
- *Six Bells, Chiddingly*
- *Snowdrop Inn, South Street, Lewes*

PART FOUR

PERFORMING HERITAGE

Sussex, despite having only a handful of big towns, has a good number of fair-sized venues thanks to the tourist trade and the enthusiasm of resident music-lovers, and there's a wide enough range of concerts and shows to cater for the tastes of most people without having to leave the county. In fact, some places, like the Brighton Dome and De la Warr Pavilion in Bexhill, bring people into Sussex, and Glyndebourne Festival Opera attracts international audiences as well as taking its productions to other parts of the country.

But the concert halls in the major towns are only the tip of a large musical iceberg. Many styles of music (and, let's not forget, a great deal of amateur music-making) would be out of place in such grand surroundings and so there are also plenty of smaller theatres and concert rooms, which are more appropriate for recitals and chamber music, and sometimes for folk and jazz too.

Big-name bands are more likely to be found at one-off outdoor events and festivals, but the majority of rock music is to be found in clubs and pubs. The same is true for jazz, folk, blues and just about everything else – not only in the towns, where there just aren't enough venues to hold the huge number of bands wanting to perform, but also deep into rural Sussex, where many pubs have exchanged their role as social meeting-place and local watering hole for one as centre of musical life.

The gap between supply of purpose-built music venues and demand for performance space has been filled not only by pubs but community centres, village halls, churches and church halls, and even one or two cricket pavilions and football stadiums.

The range of music is huge, often featuring world-class performers. Not that we should be snobbish about amateur performances – plenty of them are first-rate, and often are the stepping stone for musicians who go on to much bigger things.

GLYNDEBOURNE

DOWNLAND OPERA

The great cities of the world proudly boast the great opera houses – Milan has La Scala, New York has The Met, London has Covent Garden, and Sydney practically flaunts the most ostentatious of them all. And then there's Glyndebourne, tucked away in the Sussex Downs, miles from even the nearest town and discreetly signposted from the main roads: a world-famous opera house, in spectacular surroundings, and a unique attraction that Sussex is justifiably proud of, but in a modest, typically Sussex, sort of way.

It's not only the setting that sets Glyndebourne apart from other opera houses. It is very much a festival of opera, part of the summer 'season', rather than a year-round facility (although its activities have been expanded over the years to include Glyndebourne Touring Opera, and more recent initiatives such as less formal out-of-season performances). 'Going to Glyndebourne' is almost as much a social as an artistic treat, with a strict dress code, and taking up most of a day rather than just an evening. Performances during the season start in the afternoon but have an extended interval in which audiences are encouraged to picnic on the lawns or dine in one of the suitably upmarket restaurants in the grounds, as well as meander round the gardens and perhaps watch orchestra members playing croquet.

Glyndebourne was originally the name of a country house on the edge of the village of Glynde, five miles east of Lewes, probably built in the early 16th century. For centuries it was the home of the Hay family, until in the mid-19th century ownership passed through John Hay Langham to the Langham Christie family. Successive generations of Christies renovated and extended the property in the 1870s, and when John Christie took over the house in 1913 he continued the renovation work, including an extension in which to indulge his passion for music. The music room was a substantial addition to the house, with an impressive built-in organ of cathedral-like proportions, and enough room to host audiences for his operatic soirées.

From such small, but certainly not humble, beginnings Glyndebourne Festival Opera was born. Christie and his wife Audrey Mildmay, a soprano he had met through the Glyndebourne amateur opera evenings, decided to expand the idea into a festival of professional performances and started work on a further extension to the organ room, with stage facilities, full-sized orchestra pit and capacity for an audience of 300. The theatre was completed in 1934 and Christie was fortunate enough to be able to appoint Fritz Busch, exiled in Britain by the Nazi regime in Germany, as its first music director and Carl Ebert, who also had to flee from his post with the Berlin Opera, as artistic director.

Christie and his team agreed that the intimate auditorium was better suited to small-scale productions than grand opera but quality was not to be compromised, so it was decided that the festival should focus on the operas of Mozart. The first six-week festival opened on May 28th 1934 with *Le Nozze di Figaro*, followed the next day by *Così fan Tutte*. Needless to say, it was a success, and it soon became apparent that the auditorium was inadequate for the demand; audience capacity was increased over the years until in the 1970s it could house 850 opera-goers. Interrupted only by World War II, Glyndebourne Festival Opera ran continuously in John Christie's theatre, under the supervision of the Christie family, until 1993.

Richard D'Oyly Carte

John Christie was not the only opera impresario with links to Sussex. Richard D'Oyly Carte (1844-1901), producer of the Savoy Operas of Gilbert and Sullivan, founder of the D'Oyly Carte Opera Company, and entrepreneur behind the Savoy Theatre and Savoy Hotel, is buried in St Andrew's churchyard in Fairlight. His grave is next to those of his parents, who had moved from their London home to a house in the High Street, Old Town, Hastings.

Even with its increased capacity and the addition of a rehearsal room, the original Glyndebourne theatre couldn't keep up with the requirements of an opera house in the 1980s: demand for tickets continued to outstrip the number of seats, and ever more sophisticated productions struggled to fit into the limited backstage space. Further expansion of the building was out of the question, so in 1987 George Christie, grandson of the founder and now festival chairman, announced an ambitious new plan to replace it with a purpose-built theatre with seats for an audience of 1200. Around £34 million was raised, most of it from donations, and at the end of the 1992 season Glyndebourne's old theatre closed for the last time. The festival did not take place in 1993, but reopened in its new premises on May 28th 1994, 60 years to the day after the first opening night and with the very same opera, Mozart's *Le Nozze di Figaro*.

The new opera house was the first to be built in Britain since John Christie's original theatre, and was in keeping with Glyndebourne's tradition of introducing change to the sometimes conservative world of opera. Despite its formal, and some might say exclusive, image and retaining a core repertoire of Mozart operas, Glyndebourne has been at the forefront of innovative programming, particularly in the postwar period. Britten's *Rape of Lucretia* and *Albert Herring* were premiered there in the 1940s, and an increasing number of 20th-century operas were staged from the 1960s onwards, including Gershwin's *Porgy and Bess* directed by Trevor Nunn. In 1984 the festival adopted a policy of including a premiere performance at least every two years, starting with Oliver Knussen's *Where the Wild Things Are*, giving a platform for young composers as well as established names such as Michael Tippett. As well as promoting new works, Glyndebourne resurrected some of the very first operas, which had been neglected elsewhere: productions of Monteverdi and Cavalli classics conducted by Raymond Leppard in the 1960s introduced Venetian opera to the British stage.

The quality of these productions was second to none, featuring internationally famous soloists supported by a professional chorus and, since the 1960s, the London Philharmonic Orchestra as resident orchestra, more recently with the period-instrument Orchestra of the Age of

Enlightenment as associate orchestra. And contrary to the accusations of elitism, the formation of Glyndebourne Touring Opera in 1967 has taken productions to audiences all over Britain and given young singers the opportunity to appear alongside established performers; and recordings of many of the shows have been made commercially available on CD and DVD, broadcast on radio and TV, and most recently, screened in mainstream cinemas.

It's a long way from the private musical evenings in John Christie's music room. Still under the supervision of the Christie family, Glyndebourne's reputation rests solely on the quality of its productions (advertisements for festival tickets were not even contemplated until 2003), and has been achieved without public subsidy, largely through ticket sales and the generosity of its patrons. It's a success story Sussex can be proud of. But quietly.

Glyndebourne's Music Directors

1934-1951	Fritz Busch
1952-1963	Vittorio Gui
1964-1977	John Pritchard
1978-1988	Bernard Haitink
1989-2000	Andrew Davis
2001-	Vladimir Jurowski

The new theatre

A competition to design a new theatre for Glyndebourne laid down demanding guidelines: a large auditorium with superb acoustics but retaining the old theatre's intimacy, as well as state-of-the-art backstage and front-of-house facilities. It was a tall order, but won by Michael Hopkins and Partners with plans for an oval building made of handmade bricks, with a horseshoe-shaped auditorium fitted out with antique pine in the stalls, two balconies and a gallery and a semi-circular stage building with a steel fly-tower clad in lead and storage space for scenery. Work on the new building started in 1991, and was completed in time for the 1994 festival when it was opened to high acclaim, winning several architectural awards.

DE LA WARR PAVILION

A MODERNIST MASTERPIECE

It's hard to believe now, but genteel Bexhill-on-Sea once had a socialist Mayor. Reassuringly, he was Herbrand Edward Dundonald Brassey Sackville, ninth Earl De la Warr (which locals still pronounce as 'della war' despite being told it should be 'delaware'), the first hereditary peer to join the Labour Party and presumably the acceptable face of socialism in the 1930s. On his initiative, Bexhill council made plans to develop the central seafront and with the RIBA launched a competition for designs for a public building on the site.

The winning design came from Eric Mendelsohn and Serge Chermayeff, leading architects in the modernist style, with an ambitious plan for a multi-purpose entertainment building overlooking promenades and terraces down to the sea. Work started on the project in early 1935, and the De la Warr Pavilion was opened on December 12th that year, putting Bexhill, probably much to its surprise, firmly on the cultural map.

The building is a superb example of International-Style architecture, with large expanses of metal-framed glass in a welded steel and concrete structure, featuring south-facing balconies and roof terraces linked by a magnificent curved staircase on the seaward side and a cantilevered staircase beside the main entrance on the north side; but in addition to its outstanding aesthetic qualities, it provided a comprehensive complex of facilities – restaurant, lounge, reading room and, most importantly, a 1500-seat auditorium.

For a few brief years, the De la Warr was one of the most fashionable attractions on the south coast, with an impressive range of music in the concert hall, but this abruptly came to an end when Bexhill found itself on the front line of defence at the outbreak of World War II. The building was taken over for military use and part of the foundations were damaged by German bombing. It was going to be an uphill struggle to regain the impetus of its heyday when it reopened after the war.

The postwar years saw a gradual neglect of the building and, worse, some inappropriate alterations, under the unimaginative management of the local coucil. By the 1980s, it was in a sorry state and the programme of entertainment was equally lacklustre, but moves to save it from further deterioration were under way: it was granted Grade I listed building status in 1986, and the formation of a Pavilion Trust stimulated interest in its restoration. A grant of £6 million from the Arts Council and the Heritage Lottery Fund in 2002 enabled work to start on restoring the structure to its former glory, to be run as a centre for the arts by the De la Warr Pavilion Charitable Trust.

The Pavilion reopened after extensive renovation in 2005 and embarked on an ambitious programme in the refurbished auditorium and new gallery spaces. Widely acclaimed as an architectural triumph and praised for its exhibitions of the visual arts, it has however not yet become the Mecca for the concert-goer it might have been – but establishing such a reputation takes time and, without wishing to detract from the building as a whole, it is not quite an ideal concert hall. The auditorium is perhaps too modernistically rectilinear and lacking in warmth, both aesthetically and acoustically, for it to become a major concert venue. But this is really a minor niggle and maybe improvements can be made to the theatre as the De la Warr Pavilion grows in stature as probably the finest contemporary cultural centre in Sussex.

The bandstand

The original plans for the Pavilion (which included hotels to the north of the building, masking the blank walls) had a colonnaded bandstand on the eastern side but this was never built. An inappropriate bandstand (known locally as 'the bus shelter') was added to the terrace on the seaward terrace after World War II, and mercifully replaced in the restoration by a specially commissioned movable structure which complements the modernist style of the main building.

BRIGHTON DOME

THE DOME, CORN EXCHANGE
& PAVILION THEATRE

There has never been a shortage of concert venues in Sussex and, even though the majority are found in the string of towns along the coast, most of the county is within reasonably easy reach of a decent-sized concert hall capable of housing a full symphony orchestra. This is what they were designed for, and sadly do less and less frequently as their programmes become increasingly populist, but at least they have mostly survived the rival attractions of radio and television and now offer a wide range of musical entertainment. And many of them are fine buildings that have played a significant part in the musical life of the area.

As with everything else, Brighton, the only large city, has the most to offer. Central, in every sense, to the music scene is the Brighton Dome comprising three venues: the Dome Concert Hall, Corn Exchange and Pavilion Theatre. The Dome, once an equestrian manège, was originally built for the Prince of Wales as part of the town centre Royal Pavilion Estate in 1805. It was converted into a concert hall in 1866, then renovated in 1935 with an art-deco interior, and finally underwent a massive restoration programme which was completed in 2002. Now under the aegis of the Brighton Festival Society, the Dome caters for concert-goers from across the county, with the three auditoriums providing for all kinds of performance. The main 1850-seat Concert Hall has a year-round programme of concerts, both classical and popular, and is the home of the Brighton Philharmonic Orchestra. The Corn Exchange, once the Prince Regent's riding house, is now a versatile venue that can seat 570 people or provide standing room for more than 1000 on its sprung floor, making it ideal for smaller ensembles or informal dance and pop bands. The Pavilion Theatre can seat 220 for community events or more intimate performances.

The city centre also has the Theatre Royal, a stone's throw from the Dome, which stages musicals and variety shows, the Komedia with its three stages and club atmosphere, and the seafront Brighton Centre which can hold 4500 and therefore hosts shows by visiting major bands and orchestras, but is still rather chilly and uncomfortable. A £200 million re-fit is under discussion. In nearby Hove there is the Old Market, restored in 1999, which puts on a varied programme of music and drama, including regular appearances of the resident orchestra, The Hanover Band.

Along the coast west of Brighton, several venues merit a visit. In Worthing, for example, the unpromising-looking Assembly Hall boasts a fine acoustic, and is home to one of the few surviving south coast resort orchestras, the Worthing Symphony Orchestra, and the Pavilion Theatre also has some concerts and musicals. Bognor has a lively musical life too, largely centred on the Alexandra Theatre in the Hotham Arts Centre, but also in smaller venues such as the Regis Recital Hall in the Regis School of Music. Slightly inland, The Venue and the Assembly Rooms at Chichester offer more comfortable seating than its other main concert venue, the Cathedral.

Serving the north of the county, the main concert hall is the Hawth in Crawley, a purpose-built arts centre opened in 1988, which has staged an impressive range of concerts, opera and ballet, and has a Studio for smaller-scale shows. The Chequer Mead Theatre in East Grinstead and Clair Hall in Haywards Heath cater for mid-Sussex.

East Sussex has its share of attractions too, especially the newly-refurbished De la Warr Pavilion (*see pp. 86-87*) in Bexhill, and Eastbourne, perhaps not on such a grand scale as Brighton, nevertheless has four theatres: the Congress Theatre, which hosts concerts, opera and ballet as well as drama; the 19th-century Devonshire Park Theatre; the Winter Garden; and the Royal Hippodrome. All put on musicals and variety shows. Finally, Hastings, often thought of as the poor relation of Sussex resorts, has the White Rock Theatre opposite the pier, and for a short time also offered a splendid multi-purpose arts centre at St Mary-in-the-Castle (*see pp. 90-91*).

ST MARY-IN-THE-CASTLE

PROMENADE ELEGANCE

While the De la Warr Pavilion is undoubtedly the county's flagship arts centre, there is another Sussex architectural gem, but of an earlier era, in the church of St Mary-in-the-Castle, the centrepiece of Pelham Crescent on Hastings seafront. The area below the ruins of Hastings Castle was owned by Thomas Pelham, Earl of Chichester, in the 1820s and it was he who commissioned architect Joseph Kay to oversee its development as a crescent of houses, with a church in classical style at its centre and a colonnaded arcade on the promenade below. The project, which involved cutting into the cliff that towered over the seafront, was completed in 1828, adding a much-needed splash of elegance to the area between the new town centre and Hastings Old Town.

St Mary's remained in use as a church until the 1970s, when declining congregations and increased maintenance costs forced its closure. By 1986, it had fallen into almost terminal disrepair but was saved from demolition by Hastings Borough Council, who (after lobbying from a group of campaigners backed by Sir Hugh Casson) acquired the building and began the very expensive process of restoration. Financial support for the project came from English Heritage and later an EU grant, even though no firm plans had yet been made for its subsequent use.

Local arts groups urged the council to consider using it as an arts centre, particularly because its superb acoustics would make it an ideal concert hall, and in 1994 formed a charitable organisation, FOSMIC (Friends of St Mary-in-the-Castle), with this as their main objective. The now Grade II listed building attracted one of the first National Lottery awards over £1 million in 1995, enabling the final phase of restoration and conversion into a centre for the arts, and was leased to FOSMIC the following year, formally opening as an arts centre in 1998.

With the next-door house as office space and part of the arcade below as an entrance hall leading through an art gallery in the crypt to the main auditorium, St Mary-in-the-Castle provided a resource for local artists and performers as well as a venue for top class concerts and recitals. The main hall, seating around 500, was an ideal medium-sized auditorium with admirable acoustics, occasionally hired for recording.

Unfortunately, its glory was short-lived: run largely by volunteers from FOSMIC with a professional manager and only skeleton stage crew, it struggled to meet the demands of such a major venue, and was forced to limit the scope of its programme. The centre finally closed in 2005, amid conflicting accusations of mismanagement, lack of council and public support, and claims of prohibitive maintenance costs. In 2007, St Mary's was leased to the Sonrise Church in a very controversial deal with Hastings Council, and reverted to its original evangical role. Once again, the building had been saved, but the town had lost a great asset.

Church music

In Sussex, there is much musical activitiy in the cathedrals at Chichester and Arundel, with fine choirs and organs and suitably atmospheric acoustics, but they are by no means the only places of worship hosting concerts and recitals. In virtually every town and village across the county, both amateur and professional musicians can be heard on a regular basis in churches and even church halls. Lunchtime recitals, notably those in the Chapel Royal in Brighton, have become a feature in many town centre churches, and the absence of suitable auditoriums in rural areas has meant their increasing use for musical purposes. And for performances requiring an organ, there are very few alternatives – the recitals on the uniquely splendid Father Willis organ in All Saints, Hastings Old Town, for example, could not sensibly take place anywhere else.

John Mason Neale

While on the subject of church music in Sussex, mention has to be made of the Reverend John Mason Neale (1818-66), Warden of Sackville College in East Grinstead, who wrote 'Good King Wenceslas', 'Good Christian Men, Rejoice' and many other much-loved and well- known hymns.

END-OF-THE-PIER SHOW

Sussex has a long, south-facing coastline dotted with resorts that sprang into being with the craze for seaside holidays in the 19th century. Holiday-makers came down for the bathing and bracing sea air, but were also on the lookout for entertainment in the evenings and the days when the British weather made dipping a less than attractive prospect. The grander hotels (in fact the Grand Hotels) provided palm-court style orchestras to entertain their guests, and concert halls were built too; but as the railways made the coast available to an increasing number of less affluent visitors, staying in more modest guest-house accommodation, a new form of attraction appeared – the pier.

From Bognor to Hastings, the Victorians adorned the Sussex coast with a string of piers to cater for the new boom industry, tourism. These mainly cast-iron structures were complete entertainment complexes, with promenades, arcades and more often than not bandstands and concert halls. They were also home to summer seasons of music and shows, ranging from music-hall variety acts to classical orchestral concerts. The end-of-the-pier show had arrived.

By the turn of the century, every resort worth its salt had at least one pier (except Bexhill, where arguments about who should build it, and where, meant it never got built), and they were competing with one another to attract visitors; the piers at Bognor, Worthing, Eastbourne, St Leonards and Hastings all had fine theatres or concert halls, as did the two in Brighton, and music was a major crowd-puller. And so it went on, the only changes being the style of music, well into the 20th century. In their heyday, they even had resident orchestras – the municipal orchestras in Worthing and Hastings, and the West Pier Orchestra (conducted by Albert Ketèlbey in the 1920s) in Brighton, for example – and Bognor Pier had a novelty 'mechanical orchestra'.

But their days were numbered, for several reasons. The rise of the package holiday led to a general decline in the traditional British seaside holiday, and TV, radio and recordings had an impact on concert-going. The auditoriums on Bognor and Eastbourne piers were converted into nightclubs and Brighton's Palace Pier concert hall became a conglomeration of bars and amusement arcades. Hastings Pier Ballroom enjoyed a brief Indian Summer in the 1960s as a venue for rock concerts featuring bands as big as the Rolling Stones and the Jimi Hendrix Experience, but soon became yet another disco.

A major factor was the weather and the ravages of salt water on cast iron. The Chain Pier in Brighton, built in 1823, had already been virtually destroyed by storms by the time the Palace Pier was finished in 1899, and Brighton's West Pier, despite attempts at restoration in the 1980s, was only open from 1863 to 1975 when high maintenance costs forced its closure. The pier at St Leonards, cut in half during World War II to prevent it being used as a landing stage in a German invasion, had to be demolished in 1951, and Hastings Pier closed in 2006 when the structure was found to be dangerously corroded.

Although some of the piers remain, and are protected to some extent by conservation organisations, their musical life is all but finished. The end of an era perhaps, and certainly the end of the end-of-the-pier show.

Music alfresco

The Victorians were also very keen on outdoor performances, and have left a legacy of very fine bandstands on the seafronts and in the parks of Sussex towns, many of which are still in use today. There are also some splendid examples in town centres, notably the Horsham bandstand and the one in Queen's Square, Crawley, but it is the seaside towns that boast the most splendid varieties: Bognor Bandstand, for example, or the now much neglected seafront bandstand in Brighton, for which there are plans for renovation. The jewel in the crown, though, is at Eastbourne, with seating for 1200 – the venue for spectacular concerts with firework displays, big band and rock'n'roll nights, and a 'Last Night of the Proms'. Similar outdoor concerts are also becoming popular summer attractions in parks, the grounds of stately homes and castles as well as sports grounds all over Sussex.

FESTIVALS, FURTHER READING & WEBSITES

Some festivals

BLACK HORSE MUSIC FESTIVAL
Telham, near Battle
(Spring Bank Holiday Weekend)

BLUES ON THE FARM
Chichester (June)

LEWES GUITAR FESTIVAL (July/August)

SUNFEST FESTIVAL
Bognor Regis (July)

CHIDDINGLY FESTIVAL
Six Bells, Chiddingly (Sept/Oct)

BRIGHTON EARLY MUSIC FESTIVAL
Brighton (October)

Further reading

Sussex Women by Ann Kramer
(Snake River Press, 2007)

*Sweet Sussex: Folk Songs from the
Broadwood Collections of 1843 and
1889,* ed. Lewis Jones
(Ferret Publications)

*Miss Broadwood's Delight: Folk Songs
from Sussex and Other English
Counties* ed. Lewis Jones
(Ferret Publications)

Reminiscences of Horsham by
Henry Burstow
(Free Christian Church Book
Society,1911)

*Sussex Folk: Folksong Revival and Clubs
in Sussex* by Clive Bennett
(Country Books, 2002)

*A Song for Every Season: A Hundred Years
of a Sussex Farming Family*
(London: Heinemann, 1971)

Early to Rise: A Sussex Boyhood
(London:Heinemann, 1976)
Bob Copper's Sussex
(SB Publications, 1997)

*Across Sussex with Belloc: In the Footsteps
of the Four Men*
(Sutton Publishing, 1995)

Those Twentieth Century Blues by
Michael Tippett
(Hutchinson, 1991)

*Winifred Wagner: A Life at the Heart of
Hitler's Bayreuth* by Brigitte
Hamann (Harcourt, 2005)

*Who Killed Christopher Robin?: The Life
and Death of Brian Jones* by Terry
Rawlings (Macmillan, 1994)

Oxford Companion to Popular Music
by Peter Gammond
(Oxford University Press, 1991)

Websites

The Copper Family website
www.thecopperfamily.com/index.html

Frank Bridge
*www.musicweb-international.com/
bridge/index.htm*

The Havergal Brian Society
*www.hyperion-records.co.uk/societies/
brian.html*

John Ireland by Ian Lace
www.musicweb.uk.net/ireland/lace.htm

Eric Coates in Sussex by Ian Lace
www.musicweb.uk.net/coates/sussex.htm

INDEX

Abraham, Gerald 45
Allen, Chesney 33, 69
Amati Publishing 45
Arundel 26, 91
Attrill, George 24

Bandstands 87, 93
Bax, Arnold 34–5
Baxter, Peter 17
Bennett, Clive 27, 94
Bexhill-on-Sea 59, 61, 86–7
Blake, Howard 73
Blann, Michael 24
Bognor Regis 74, 89, 92, 93
Brian, Havergal 48–9, 94
Bridge, Frank 42–3
Brighton
    classical 42, 55, 58, 64, 65
    folk clubs 27
    popular music
        68, 69, 70, 71, 73, 74, 75, 78, 79
    venues 64, 78, 88–9, 92, 93
Britten, Benjamin 42, 43, 55
Broadwood Collection 14–15, 16, 94
Brown, Arthur 75
Burstow, Henry 16, 17
Butt, Clara 58, 60

Carroll, Lianne 71
Carter, Sydney Bertram 55
Chacksfield, Frank 69
Chichester
    classical 31–3, 47, 64–5, 91
    folk club 26
    popular music 69
    venues 89
Chiddingly folk club 27
church music 31, 50–1, 91
cinema, popular music 73
classical music 28–65
    academic institutions 54–5
    festivals 47, 62–3, 65
    instruments 45, 59
    magazines 44–5, 48
    orchestral virtuosi 58–9

orchestras/choirs 64–5, 88, 92
    women 60–1
Coates, Eric 72
Cogan, Alma 74
Collins, Shirley and Dolly 25
Conway, Russ 74
Copper family 17–21, 24, 55, 94
Crawley 27, 78, 79, 93

Davis, Colin 55, 58
De La Warr Pavilion 86–7
Debussy, Claude 37
Deller, Alfred and Mark 59
Denny, Louise 61
Dome complex, Brighton 64, 78, 88
Donaldson, John 71

East Grinstead 62, 65, 77, 89, 91
Eastbourne
        26, 27, 37, 61, 65, 74, 89, 92, 93
Elgar, Sir Edward 39, 60
Emerson, Keith 75

Faith, Adam 74
Fawkes, Wally 'Trog' 70
festivals 27, 47, 62–3, 65, 94
Finnissy, Michael 54, 56–7
Flowers, Herbie 71
folk music 12–27, 40
    clubs and festivals 25–6
    song lyrics 22–3
    Sussex revival 24–5
Frith, Fred and Simon 75

Genockey, Liam 25, 71
Gillette, Noah 24
Gipps, Ruth 61
Glyndebourne 65, 82–5
Gonella, Nat 70
Grainer, Ron 73
Grainger, Percy 15, 40–1

Hall, Mabs and Gordon 17
Hall, Reg 25, 54–5
Hamer, Ian 71
Harvey, Jonathan 50, 51–3, 54

Hastings
    classical music
        57, 58, 59, 62, 65, 83, 91
    folk 25
    popular music 69, 70, 71, 79
    venues 89, 90–1, 92, 93
Hayes, Morgan 57
Hazlewood, Charles 55, 58
Henderson, Gavin 55
Holst, Gustav 33, 47
Horsham 14, 16–17, 26, 55, 65, 93
Hove 49, 58, 68, 89
Hutchings, Ashley 25

Ireland, John 36–7, 94

Jazz 70–1, 78–9
Johnson, John 24
Jones, Brian 76–7, 94

Katin, Peter 59
Knight, Peter 25

Led Zeppelin 77
Lee, Kate 18
Lewes 26, 27, 55, 64, 75, 76
Love, Geoff 69
Lynn, Vera 69

Maynard, George 'Pop' 24
Mayne, Ernie 68
McCartney, Paul 55, 74
Merrick, W. Percy 15, 16
Miller, Max 68
Morris dancing 27
music halls 68–9, 78, 92

Neale, Revd John Mason 91
Noble, Ray 69
Norris, David Owen 59

Opera 65, 82–5

Parish, Revd W.D. 14
Parry, Charles Hubert Hastings 38
Pears, Peter 55, 58–9
Peers, Donald 74
Petworth 39, 45, 65
piers 92–3

Quilter, Roger 41, 49

Radio, popular music 69, 72–3
rock and pop 74–5, 79
Rolling Stones 76
Rottingdean 18, 19, 35
Rye 59, 65, 74

Sayer, Leo 74
Scott, Cyril 9, 41
Seabrook, Terry 71
Sharp, Cecil 13, 15
Shoreham-by-Sea 48, 49, 68, 74
Simkins, Geoff 71
Smith, Judge 75
Smith, Ronald 59
Spicer, George 'Spike' 24
St Leonards-on-Sea 44, 59, 61, 92, 93
St Mary-in-the-Castle 89, 90–1
Steyning 56
Stomp 75
Sussex by the Sea 10–11
Sussex University 52–3, 54–5

Taverner, John 50–1, 53
television, popular music 73
Tester, Lewis 'Scan' 24–5
Tilley, Vesta 68
Tippett, Michael 46–7, 84, 94
Turges/Sturges family 33
Turner, Michael 17

Variety shows 68–9, 78, 92
Vaughan Williams, Ralph 15–17, 34–5
venues 78–9, 82–93
Verrall, Harriet 16

Wagner, Winifred 62–3, 94
Wales, Tony 17, 26
Walker, Robert 39
Ward-Higgs, William 10
Warnham 17
Washington 26, 37
Watts, Trevor 71
Weelkes, Thomas 30–3
Welch, Bruce 74
Wellins, Bobby 71
West Chiltington, folk club 26
Wigglesworth, Mark 58
Williams, Billy 68
Williams, Charles 72
Willison, David 59
Woodhouse, Violet Gordon 60
Worthing 64, 72, 74–5, 78, 89, 92